I0421129

Quote Octopus
Melbourne, Victoria, 3053
Australia
www.quoteoctopus.com

Creativity is allowing yourself to make mistakes. Art is knowing which ones to keep.

Scott Adams

The purpose of art is washing the dust of daily life off our souls.

Pablo Picasso

This world is but a canvas to our imagination.

Henry David Thoreau

If you hear a voice within you say 'you cannot paint,' then by all means paint, and that voice will be silenced.

Vincent Van Gogh

A room hung with pictures is a room hung with thoughts.

Joshua Reynolds

Every picture shows a spot with which the artist has fallen in love.

Alfred Sisley

Vision is the art of seeing what is invisible to others.

Jonathan Swift

The artist is a receptacle for emotions that come from all over the place: from the sky, from the earth, from a scrap of paper, from a passing shape, from a spider's web.

Pablo Picasso

Photography takes an instant out of time, altering life by holding it still.

Dorothea Lange

I found I could say things with color and shapes that I couldn't say any other way - things I had no words for.

Georgia O'Keeffe

Wherever art appears, life disappears.

Robert Motherwell

Every artist writes his own autobiography.

Havelock Ellis

An artist must be free to choose what he does, certainly, but he must also never be afraid to do what he might choose.

Langston Hughes

Art is like a border of flowers along the course of civilization.

Lincoln Steffens

The art of art, the glory of expression and the sunshine of the light of letters, is simplicity.

Walt Whitman

If art is to nourish the roots of our culture, society must set the artist free to follow his vision wherever it takes him.

John F. Kennedy

Art enables us to find ourselves and lose ourselves at the same time.

Thomas Merton

Art, like morality, consists in drawing the line somewhere.

Gilbert K. Chesterton

Photography is a major force in explaining man to man.

Edward Steichen

Drawing is the honesty of the art. There is no possibility of cheating. It is either good or bad.

Salvador Dali

No great artist ever sees things as they really are. If he did, he would cease to be an artist.

Oscar Wilde

Art is the most intense mode of individualism that the world has known.

Oscar Wilde

One eye sees, the other feels.

Paul Klee

Writing, to me, is simply thinking through my fingers.

Isaac Asimov

Great art picks up where nature ends.

Marc Chagall

The essence of all beautiful art, all great art, is gratitude.

Friedrich Nietzsche

I have no fear of making changes, destroying the image, etc., because the painting has a life of its own.

Jackson Pollock

I don't paint things. I only paint the difference between things.

Henri Matisse

Every artist was first an amateur.

Ralph Waldo Emerson

Art is the desire of a man to express himself, to record the reactions of his personality to the world he lives in.

Amy Lowell

You don't take a photograph, you make it.

Ansel Adams

Great art is an instant arrested in eternity.

James Huneker

Art is not a handicraft, it is the transmission of feeling the artist has experienced.

Leo Tolstoy

I do not want art for a few any more than education for a few, or freedom for a few.

William Morris

I don't want to be interesting. I want to be good.

Ludwig Mies van der Rohe

Art is a harmony parallel with nature.

Paul Cezanne

Without tradition, art is a flock of sheep without a shepherd. Without innovation, it is a corpse.

Winston Churchill

Every artist dips his brush in his own soul, and paints his own nature into his pictures.

Henry Ward Beecher

In art as in love, instinct is enough.

Anatole France

Art evokes the mystery without which the world would not exist.

Rene Magritte

Painting is just another way of keeping a diary.

Pablo Picasso

Painting is an infinitely minute part of my personality.

Salvador Dali

Advertising is the greatest art form of the 20th century.

Marshall McLuhan

Contrary to general belief, an artist is never ahead of his time but most people are far behind theirs.

Edgard Varese

To create one's world in any of the arts takes courage.

Georgia O'Keeffe

The artist is nothing without the gift, but the gift is nothing without work.

Emile Zola

When I think of art I think of beauty. Beauty is the mystery of life. It is not in the eye it is in the mind. In our minds there is awareness of perfection.

Agnes Martin

Art is the unceasing effort to compete with the beauty of flowers - and never succeeding.

Gian Carlo Menotti

When one paints an ideal, one does not need to limit one's imagination.

Ellen Key

Painting is easy when you don't know how, but very difficult when you do.

Edgar Degas

Impressionism is the newspaper of the soul.

Henri Matisse

A line is a dot that went for a walk.

Paul Klee

Drawing is like making an expressive gesture with the advantage of permanence.

Henri Matisse

An artist is somebody who produces things that people don't need to have.

Andy Warhol

I'm afraid that if you look at a thing long enough, it loses all of its meaning.

Andy Warhol

Art is the only way to run away without leaving home.

Twyla Tharp

The moment you cheat for the sake of beauty, you know you're an artist.

David Hockney

Art is one thing that can go on mattering once it has stopped hurting.

Elizabeth Bowen

To an engineer, good enough means perfect. With an artist, there's no such thing as perfect.

Alexander Calder

A guilty conscience needs to confess. A work of art is a confession.

Albert Camus

Fine art is that in which the hand, the head, and the heart of man go together.

John Ruskin

There is nothing worse than a sharp image of a fuzzy concept.

Ansel Adams

I am enough of an artist to draw freely upon my imagination.

Albert Einstein

Not everybody trusts paintings but people believe photographs.

Ansel Adams

When I am finishing a picture, I hold some God-made object up to it - a rock, a flower, the branch of a tree or my hand - as a final test. If the painting stands up beside a thing man cannot make, the painting is authentic. If there's a clash between the two, it's bad art.

Marc Chagall

To send light into the darkness of men's hearts - such is the duty of the artist.

Robert Schumann

Without art, the crudeness of reality would make the world unbearable.

George Bernard Shaw

In art, the hand can never execute anything higher than the heart can imagine.

Ralph Waldo Emerson

Lying in bed would be an altogether perfect and supreme experience if only one had a colored pencil long enough to draw on the ceiling.

Gilbert K. Chesterton

An artist's only concern is to shoot for some kind of perfection, and on his own terms, not anyone else's.

J. D. Salinger

All art is autobiographical. The pearl is the oyster's autobiography.

Federico Fellini

The works must be conceived with fire in the soul but executed with clinical coolness.

Joan Miro

To be an artist includes much; one must possess many gifts - absolute gifts - which have not been acquired by one's own effort. And, moreover, to succeed, the artist much possess the courageous soul.

Kate Chopin

I cry out for order and find it only in art.

Helen Hayes

Very few people possess true artistic ability. It is therefore both unseemly and unproductive to irritate the situation by making an effort. If you have a burning, restless urge to write or paint, simply eat something sweet and the feeling will pass.

Fran Lebowitz

Art doesn't transform. It just plain forms.

Roy Lichtenstein

The artist who aims at perfection in everything achieves it in nothing.

Eugene Delacroix

When I judge art, I take my painting and put it next to a God made object like a tree or flower. If it clashes, it is not art.

Paul Cezanne

Art is either plagiarism or revolution.

Paul Gauguin

Every painting is a voyage into a sacred harbour.

Giotto di Bondone

Art, in itself, is an attempt to bring order out of chaos.

Stephen Sondheim

Art is not a study of positive reality, it is the seeking for ideal truth.

John Ruskin

To me, photography is the simultaneous recognition, in a fraction of a second, of the significance of an event.

Henri Cartier-Bresson

Art has to move you and design does not, unless it's a good design for a bus.

David Hockney

A writer should write with his eyes and a painter paint with his ears.

Gertrude Stein

Every good painter paints what he is.

Jackson Pollock

Good art is art that allows you to enter it from a variety of angles and to emerge with a variety of views.

Mary Schmich

Art is a collaboration between God and the artist, and the less the artist does the better.

Andre Gide

Immature artists imitate. Mature artists steal.

Lionel Trilling

Some painters transform the sun into a yellow spot, others transform a yellow spot into the sun.

Pablo Picasso

If you do not breathe through writing, if you do not cry out in writing, or sing in writing, then don't write, because our culture has no use for it.

Anais Nin

True art is characterized by an irresistible urge in the creative artist.

Albert Einstein

What makes photography a strange invention is that its primary raw materials are light and time.

John Berger

Art is the daughter of freedom.

Friedrich Schiller

My hand is the extension of the thinking process - the creative process.

Tadao Ando

The highest art is always the most religious, and the greatest artist is always a devout person.

Abraham Lincoln

A work of art is the unique result of a unique temperament.

Oscar Wilde

All art is but imitation of nature.

Lucius Annaeus Seneca

Abstract art: a product of the untalented sold by the unprincipled to the utterly bewildered.

Al Capp

Every production of an artist should be the expression of an adventure of his soul.

W. Somerset Maugham

Art is the stored honey of the human soul, gathered on wings of misery and travail.

Theodore Dreiser

You can't do sketches enough. Sketch everything and keep your curiosity fresh.

John Singer Sargent

I like to pretend that my art has nothing to do with me.

Roy Lichtenstein

Art is a revolt against fate. All art is a revolt against man's fate.

Andre Malraux

What art offers is space - a certain breathing room for the spirit.

John Updike

Ads are the cave art of the twentieth century.

Marshall McLuhan

The beauty one can find in art is one of the pitifully few real and lasting products of human endeavor.

J. Paul Getty

The sculptor produces the beautiful statue by chipping away such parts of the marble block as are not needed - it is a process of elimination.

Elbert Hubbard

Art is nature speeded up and God slowed down.

Malcolm de Chazal

Impressionism; it is the birth of Light in painting.

Robert Delaunay

To make us feel small in the right way is a function of art; men can only make us feel small in the wrong way.

E. M. Forster

Art begins with resistance - at the point where resistance is overcome. No human masterpiece has ever been created without great labor.

Andre Gide

A work of art has no importance whatever to society. It is only important to the individual.

Vladimir Nabokov

Art must take reality by surprise.

Francoise Sagan

A painting that is well composed is half finished.

Pierre Bonnard

Vitality is radiated from exceptional art and architecture.

Arthur Erickson

Murals in restaurants are on a par with the food in museums.

Peter De Vries

Art is the final cunning of the human soul which would rather do anything than face the gods.

Iris Murdoch

Painting seems like some kind of peculiar miracle that I need to have again and again.

Philip Guston

An artist never really finishes his work, he merely abandons it.

Paul Valery

Art is a step from what is obvious and well-known toward what is arcane and concealed.

Khalil Gibran

Art is not a thing; it is a way.

Elbert Hubbard

Art consists of limitation. The most beautiful part of every picture is the frame.

Gilbert K. Chesterton

The creative act lasts but a brief moment, a lightning instant of give-and-take, just long enough for you to level the camera and to trap the fleeting prey in your little box.

Henri Cartier-Bresson

Every human is an artist. The dream of your life is to make beautiful art.

Miguel Angel Ruiz

The very essence of the creative is its novelty, and hence we have no standard by which to judge it.

Carl Rogers

A sculptor is a person who is interested in the shape of things, a poet in words, a musician by sounds.

Henry Moore

I've been called many names like perfectionist, difficult and obsessive. I think it takes obsession, takes searching for the details for any artist to be good.

Barbra Streisand

In a decaying society, art, if it is truthful, must also reflect decay. And unless it wants to break faith with its social function, art must show the world as changeable. And help to change it.

Ernst Fischer

Photograph: a picture painted by the sun without instruction in art.

Ambrose Bierce

We have art in order not to die of the truth.

Friedrich Nietzsche

All good art is an indiscretion.

Tennessee Williams

Every time a student walks past a really urgent, expressive piece of architecture that belongs to his college, it can help reassure him that he does have that mind, does have that soul.

Louis Kahn

An artist is not paid for his labor but for his vision.

James Whistler

To say that a work of art is good, but incomprehensible to the majority of men, is the same as saying of some kind of food that it is very good but that most people can't eat it.

Leo Tolstoy

The artist produces for the liberation of his soul. It is his nature to create as it is the nature of water to run down the hill.

W. Somerset Maugham

What I wish to show when I paint is the way I see things with my eyes and in my heart.

Raoul Dufy

My painting does not come from the easel.

Jackson Pollock

You begin with the possibilities of the material.

Robert Rauschenberg

Every other artist begins with a blank canvas, a piece of paper the photographer begins with the finished product.

Edward Steichen

It may be that the deep necessity of art is the examination of self-deception.

Robert Motherwell

In art the best is good enough.

Johann Wolfgang von Goethe

Art is magic delivered from the lie of being truth.

Theodor Adorno

I don't believe in art. I believe in artists.

Marcel Duchamp

Art produces ugly things which frequently become more beautiful with time. Fashion, on the other hand, produces beautiful things which always become ugly with time.

Jean Cocteau

I choose a block of marble and chop off whatever I don't need.

Auguste Rodin

It is a mistake for a sculptor or a painter to speak or write very often about his job. It releases tension needed for his work.

Henry Moore

I paint with shapes.

Alexander Calder

A good painting to me has always been like a friend. It keeps me company, comforts and inspires.

Hedy Lamarr

An artist cannot fail; it is a success to be one.

Charles Horton Cooley

Treat a work of art like a prince. Let it speak to you first.

Arthur Schopenhauer

Lesser artists borrow, great artists steal.

Igor Stravinsky

All great art is born of the metropolis.

Ezra Pound

Painting is by nature a luminous language.

Robert Delaunay

The history of modern art is also the history of the progressive loss of art's audience. Art has increasingly become the concern of the artist and the bafflement of the public.

Paul Gauguin

The artist one day falls through a hole in the brambles, and from that moment he is following the dark rapids of an underground river which may sometimes flow so near to the surface that the laughing picnic parties are heard above.

Cyril Connolly

Pictures must not be too picturesque.

Ralph Waldo Emerson

The essence of all art is to have pleasure in giving pleasure.

Dale Carnegie

Fashion is only the attempt to realize art in living forms and social intercourse.

Francis Bacon

Painting, n.: The art of protecting flat surfaces from the weather, and exposing them to the critic.

Ambrose Bierce

Artists who seek perfection in everything are those who cannot attain it in anything.

Gustave Flaubert

An artist is a dreamer consenting to dream of the actual world.

George Santayana

The terrifying and edible beauty of Art Nouveau architecture.

Salvador Dali

Every creator painfully experiences the chasm between his inner vision and its ultimate expression.

Isaac Bashevis Singer

The principles of true art is not to portray, but to evoke.

Jerzy Kosinski

Of all lies, art is the least untrue.

Gustave Flaubert

My imagination can picture no fairer happiness than to continue living for art.

Clara Schumann

Art is the right hand of Nature. The latter has only given us being, the former has made us men.

Friedrich Schiller

An artist cannot speak about his art any more than a plant can discuss horticulture.

Jean Cocteau

The business of art is to reveal the relation between man and his environment.

D. H. Lawrence

I've never really had a hobby, unless you count art, which the IRS once told me I had to declare as a hobby since I hadn't made money with it.

Laurie Anderson

If a building becomes architecture, then it is art.

Arne Jacobsen

The artist's world is limitless. It can be found anywhere, far from where he lives or a few feet away. It is always on his doorstep.

Paul Strand

Art hurts. Art urges voyages - and it is easier to stay at home.

Gwendolyn Brooks

I will preach with my brush.

Henry Ossawa Tanner

Without freedom, no art; art lives only on the restraints it imposes on itself, and dies of all others.

Albert Camus

Personality is everything in art and poetry.

Johann Wolfgang von Goethe

The mediator of the inexpressible is the work of art.

Johann Wolfgang von Goethe

If we could but paint with the hand what we see with the eye.

Honore de Balzac

I think you can leave the arts, superior or inferior, to the conscience of mankind.

William Butler Yeats

Art for art's sake is a philosophy of the well-fed.

Frank Lloyd Wright

Rules and models destroy genius and art.

William Hazlitt

Art is man's expression of his joy in labor.

Henry A. Kissinger

I don't want life to imitate art. I want life to be art.

Ernst Fischer

So vast is art, so narrow human wit.

Alexander Pope

A work of art that contains theories is like an object on which the price tag has been left.

Alexander Pope

The waking mind is the least serviceable in the arts.

Henry Miller

The task of art today is to bring chaos into order.

Theodor Adorno

Even a true artist does not always produce art.

Carroll O'Connor

Pictures deface walls more often than they decorate them.

William Wordsworth

Art is parasitic on life, just as criticism is parasitic on art.

Harry S Truman

A great artist is always before his time or behind it.

George Edward Moore

Art is science made clear.

Wilson Mizner

My love of fine art increased - the more of it I saw, the more of it I wanted to see.

J. Paul Getty

The principle of art is to pause, not bypass.

Jerzy Kosinski

Beauty in art is often nothing but ugliness subdued.

Jean Rostand

My eyes were made to erase all that is ugly.

Raoul Dufy

Time extracts various values from a painter's work. When these values are exhausted the pictures are forgotten, and the more a picture has to give, the greater it is.

Henri Matisse

Art is the concrete representation of our most subtle feelings.

Agnes Martin

Summer is a great time to visit art museums, which offer the refreshing rinse of swimming pools - only instead of cool water, you immerse yourself in art.

Jerry Saltz

That's the motivation of an artist - to seek attention of some kind.

James Taylor

To make pictures big is to make them more powerful.

Robert Mapplethorpe

When that shutter clicks, anything else that can be done afterward is not worth consideration.

Edward Steichen

Modern art is what happens when painters stop looking at girls and persuade themselves that they have a better idea.

John Ciardi

An empty canvas is full.

Robert Rauschenberg

Culture is the arts elevated to a set of beliefs.

Thomas Wolfe

Paint the essential character of things.

Camille Pissarro

The more horrifying this world becomes, the more art becomes abstract.

Ellen Key

Mournful and yet grand is the destiny of the artist.

Franz Liszt

Artists themselves are not confined, but their output is.

Robert Smithson

Great artists suffer for the people.

Marvin Gaye

In an artwork you're always looking for artistic decisions, so an ashtray is perfect. An ashtray has got life and death.

Damien Hirst

Art ought never to be considered except in its relations with its ideal beauty.

Alfred de Vigny

I think of my peace paintings as one long poem, with each painting being a single stanza.

Robert Indiana

My attitude towards drawing is not necessarily about drawing. It's about making the best kind of image I can make, it's about talking as clearly as I can.

Jim Dine

I was the least Pop of all the Pop artists.

Robert Indiana

Artists don't make objects. Artists make mythologies.

Anish Kapoor

The writer, when he is also an artist, is someone who admits what others don't dare reveal.

Elia Kazan

The history of art is the history of revivals.

Samuel Butler

Works of art, in my opinion, are the only objects in the material universe to possess internal order, and that is why, though I don't believe that only art matters, I do believe in Art for Art's sake.

E. M. Forster

When I work, and in my art, I hold hands with God.

Robert Mapplethorpe

I don't think there's any artist of any value who doesn't doubt what they're doing.

Francis Ford Coppola

The arts are an even better barometer of what is happening in our world than the stock market or the debates in congress.

Hendrik Willem Van Loon

Trying to force creativity is never good.

Sarah McLachlan

I think an artist's responsibility is more complex than people realize.

Jodie Foster

Art is an invention of aesthetics, which in turn is an invention of philosophers... What we call art is a game.

Octavio Paz

Art in Nature is rhythmic and has a horror of constraint.

Robert Delaunay

The Japanese have a wonderful sense of design and a refinement in their art. They try to produce beautiful paintings with the minimum number of strokes.

David Rockefeller

Rationalism is the enemy of art, though necessary as a basis for architecture.

Arthur Erickson

I realize that protest paintings are not exactly in vogue, but I've done many.

Robert Indiana

It is art that makes life, makes interest, makes importance and I know of no substitute whatever for the force and beauty of its process.

Max Eastman

No heirloom of humankind captures the past as do art and language.

Theodore Bikel

Art is subject to arbitrary fashion.

Kary Mullis

When I make art, I think about its ability to connect with others, to bring them into the process.

Jim Hodges

I'm not gonna give the British Government the joy of keeping taxing me. They don't tax art. And all my cars are just a collection of art.

Jay Kay

Art depends on luck and talent.

Francis Ford Coppola

The vitality of a new movement in Art must be gauged by the fury it arouses.

Logan Pearsall Smith

The hours I spend with you I look upon as sort of a perfumed garden, a dim twilight, and a fountain singing to it. You and you alone make me feel that I am alive. Other men it is said have seen angels, but I have seen thee and thou art enough.

George Edward Moore

Sometimes being a friend means mastering the art of timing. There is a time for silence. A time to let go and allow people to hurl themselves into their own destiny. And a time to prepare to pick up the pieces when it's all over.

Octavia Butler

Procrastination is the art of keeping up with yesterday.

Don Marquis

Oh, if it be to choose and call thee mine, love, thou art every day my Valentine!

Thomas Hood

It is the supreme art of the teacher to awaken joy in creative expression and knowledge.

Albert Einstein

The supreme art of war is to subdue the enemy without fighting.

Sun Tzu

Beautiful music is the art of the prophets that can calm the agitations of the soul; it is one of the most magnificent and delightful presents God has given us.

Martin Luther

Vulnerability is the essence of romance. It's the art of being uncalculated, the willingness to look foolish, the courage to say, 'This is me, and I'm interested in you enough to show you my flaws with the hope that you may embrace me for all that I am but, more important, all that I am not.'

Ashton Kutcher

Be true to yourself, help others, make each day your masterpiece, make friendship a fine art, drink deeply from good books - especially the Bible, build a shelter against a rainy day, give thanks for your blessings and pray for guidance every day.

John Wooden

Friendship is unnecessary, like philosophy, like art... It has no survival value; rather it is one of those things that give value to survival.

C. S. Lewis

Architecture is the art of how to waste space.

Philip Johnson

You must not fight too often with one enemy, or you will teach him all your art of war.

Napoleon Bonaparte

Simplicity is natures first step, and the last of art.

Philip James Bailey

Love of beauty is taste. The creation of beauty is art.

Ralph Waldo Emerson

Good management is the art of making problems so interesting and their solutions so constructive that everyone wants to get to work and deal with them.

Paul Hawken

I have seen many storms in my life. Most storms have caught me by surprise, so I had to learn very quickly to look further and understand that I am not capable of controlling the weather, to exercise the art of patience and to respect the fury of nature.

Paulo Coelho

Next to the Word of God, the noble art of music is the greatest treasure in the world.

Martin Luther

Motivation is the art of getting people to do what you want them to do because they want to do it.

Dwight D. Eisenhower

The art of love is largely the art of persistence.

Albert Ellis

All married couples should learn the art of battle as they should learn the art of making love. Good battle is objective and honest - never vicious or cruel. Good battle is healthy and constructive, and brings to a marriage the principles of equal partnership.

Ann Landers

To me, photography is an art of observation. It's about finding something interesting in an ordinary place... I've found it has little to do with the things you see and everything to do with the way you see them.

Elliott Erwitt

The art of writing is the art of discovering what you believe.

Gustave Flaubert

The mother art is architecture. Without an architecture of our own we have no soul of our own civilization.

Frank Lloyd Wright

In our life there is a single color, as on an artist's palette, which provides the meaning of life and art. It is the color of love.

Marc Chagall

It is not up to me whether I win or lose. Ultimately, this might not be my day. And it is that philosophy towards sports, something that I really truly live by. I am emotional. I want to win. I am hungry. I am a competitor. I have that fire. But deep down, I truly enjoy the art of competing so much more than the result.

Apolo Ohno

The art of teaching is the art of assisting discovery.

Mark Van Doren

Custom, that is before all law; Nature, that is above all art.

Samuel Daniel

Feelings aroused by the touch of someone's hand, the sound of music, the smell of a flower, a beautiful sunset, a work of art, love, laughter, hope and faith - all work on both the unconscious and the conscious aspects of the self, and they have physiological consequences as well.

Bernie Siegel

Creative without strategy is called 'art.' Creative with strategy is called 'advertising.'

Jef I. Richards

Making money is art and working is art and good business is the best art.

Andy Warhol

Riding a race bike is an art - a thing that you do because you feel something inside.

Valentino Rossi

Politics is the art of looking for trouble, finding it everywhere, diagnosing it incorrectly and applying the wrong remedies.

Groucho Marx

Life is the art of drawing without an eraser.

John W. Gardner

The most beautiful thing we can experience is the mysterious. It is the source of all true art and science.

Albert Einstein

Diversity: the art of thinking independently together.

Malcolm Forbes

The art of war is simple enough. Find out where your enemy is. Get at him as soon as you can. Strike him as hard as you can, and keep moving on.

Ulysses S. Grant

Be true to yourself. Make each day a masterpiece. Help others. Drink deeply from good books. Make friendship a fine art. Build a shelter against a rainy day.

John Wooden

Tact is the art of making a point without making an enemy.

Isaac Newton

Every bit of me is devoted to love and art. And I aspire to try to be a teacher to my young fans who feel just like I felt when I was younger. I just felt like a freak. I guess what I'm trying to say is I'm trying to liberate them, I want to free them of their fears and make them feel that they can make their own space in the world.

Lady Gaga

Were I called on to define, very briefly, the term Art, I should call it 'the reproduction of what the Senses perceive in Nature through the veil of the soul.' The mere imitation, however accurate, of what is in Nature, entitles no man to the sacred name of 'Artist.'

Edgar Allan Poe

Don't only practice your art, but force your way into its secrets; art deserves that, for it and knowledge can raise man to the Divine.

Ludwig van Beethoven

'Crazy' is a term of art; 'Insane' is a term of law. Remember that, and you will save yourself a lot of trouble.

Hunter S. Thompson

Art is never finished, only abandoned.

Leonardo da Vinci

Design is the method of putting form and content together. Design, just as art, has multiple definitions; there is no single definition. Design can be art. Design can be aesthetics. Design is so simple, that's why it is so complicated.

Paul Rand

Originality is the fine art of remembering what you hear but forgetting where you heard it.

Laurence J. Peter

Blue thou art, intensely blue; Flower, whence came thy dazzling hue?

James Montgomery

Science fiction is any idea that occurs in the head and doesn't exist yet, but soon will, and will change everything for everybody, and nothing will ever be the same again. As soon as you have an idea that changes some small part of the world you are writing science fiction. It is always the art of the possible, never the impossible.

Ray Bradbury

Even in literature and art, no man who bothers about originality will ever be original: whereas if you simply try to tell the truth (without caring twopence how often it has been told before) you will, nine times out of ten, become original without ever having noticed it.

C. S. Lewis

Photography is more than a medium for factual communication of ideas. It is a creative art.

Ansel Adams

The art of living is more like wrestling than dancing.

Marcus Aurelius

Literature is the art of discovering something extraordinary about ordinary people, and saying with ordinary words something extraordinary.

Boris Pasternak

I consider skateboarding an art form, a lifestyle and a sport. 'Action sport' would be the least offensive categorization.

Tony Hawk

The art of being happy lies in the power of extracting happiness from common things.

Henry Ward Beecher

One of the most amazing things about mathematics is the people who do math aren't usually interested in application, because mathematics itself is truly a beautiful art form. It's structures and patterns, and that's what we love, and that's what we get off on.

Danica McKellar

Mathematics is the art of giving the same name to different things.

Henri Poincare

Advertising is the art of convincing people to spend money they don't have for something they don't need.

Will Rogers

Well, Art is Art, isn't it? Still, on the other hand, water is water. And east is east and west is west and if you take cranberries and stew them like applesauce they taste much more like prunes than rhubarb does. Now you tell me what you know.

Groucho Marx

Architecture is a visual art, and the buildings speak for themselves.

Julia Morgan

A great city, whose image dwells in the memory of man, is the type of some great idea. Rome represents conquest; Faith hovers over the towers of Jerusalem; and Athens embodies the pre-eminent quality of the antique world, Art.

Benjamin Disraeli

Animation is not the art of drawings that move but the art of movements that are drawn.

Norman McLaren

Leadership is the art of getting someone else to do something you want done because he wants to do it.

Dwight D. Eisenhower

In mathematics the art of proposing a question must be held of higher value than solving it.

Georg Cantor

Medicine is a science of uncertainty and an art of probability.

William Osler

People discuss my art and pretend to understand as if it were necessary to understand, when it's simply necessary to love.

Claude Monet

The art of simplicity is a puzzle of complexity.

Douglas Horton

Errors are not in the art but in the artificers.

Isaac Newton

It's very important that we re-learn the art of resting and relaxing. Not only does it help prevent the onset of many illnesses that develop through chronic tension and worrying; it allows us to clear our minds, focus, and find creative solutions to problems.

Thich Nhat Hanh

O, thou art fairer than the evening air clad in the beauty of a thousand stars.

Christopher Marlowe

I never called my work an 'art'. It's part of show business, the business of building entertainment.

Walt Disney

Advertising is fundamentally persuasion and persuasion happens to be not a science, but an art.

William Bernbach

Music is God's gift to man, the only art of Heaven given to earth, the only art of earth we take to Heaven.

Walter Savage Landor

I regard the theatre as the greatest of all art forms, the most immediate way in which a human being can share with another the sense of what it is to be a human being.

Thornton Wilder

Youth is the gift of nature, but age is a work of art.

Stanislaw Jerzy Lec

The human foot is a masterpiece of engineering and a work of art.

Leonardo da Vinci

There is no abstract art. You must always start with something. Afterward you can remove all traces of reality.

Pablo Picasso

Dying is an art, like everything else. I do it exceptionally well. I do it so it feels like hell. I do it so it feels real. I guess you could say I've a call.

Sylvia Plath

What I dream of is an art of balance, of purity and serenity devoid of troubling or depressing subject matter - a soothing, calming influence on the mind, rather like a good armchair which provides relaxation from physical fatigue.

Henri Matisse

Our individual lives cannot, generally, be works of art unless the social order is also.

Charles Horton Cooley

Art is what you can get away with.

Andy Warhol

The art of photography is all about directing the attention of the viewer.

Steven Pinker

Logic: The art of thinking and reasoning in strict accordance with the limitations and incapacities of the human misunderstanding.

Ambrose Bierce

You use a glass mirror to see your face; you use works of art to see your soul.

George Bernard Shaw

Building art is a synthesis of life in materialised form. We should try to bring in under the same hat not a splintered way of thinking, but all in harmony together.

Alvar Aalto

The art of communication is the language of leadership.

James Humes

Pop Art looks out into the world. It doesn't look like a painting of something, it looks like the thing itself.

Roy Lichtenstein

Professionalism in art has this difficulty: To be professional is to be dependable, to be dependable is to be predictable, and predictability is esthetically boring - an anti-virtue in a field where we hope to be astonished and startled and at some deep level refreshed.

John Updike

Language is a social art.

Willard Van Orman Quine

Find a beautiful piece of art. If you fall in love with Van Gogh or Matisse or John Oliver Killens, or if you fall love with the music of Coltrane, the music of Aretha Franklin, or the music of Chopin - find some beautiful art and admire it, and realize that that was created by human beings just like you, no more human, no less.

Maya Angelou

You cannot live to please everyone else. You have to edify, educate and fulfill your own dreams and destiny, and hope that whatever your art is that you're putting out there, if it's received, great, I respect you for receiving it. If it's not received, great, I respect you for not.

Octavia Spencer

I'm free. I just do what I want, say what I want, say how I feel, and I don't try to hurt nobody. I just try to make sure that I don't compromise my art in any kind of way, and I think people respect that.

Erykah Badu

I try to give people a different way of looking at their surroundings. That's art to me.

Maya Lin

Art is not what you see, but what you make others see.

Edgar Degas

It'll be the Internet and piracy that will kill film. There's a philosophy that the Internet should be free, but the reality is that piracy will destroy the film industry and film as an art form because it's expensive to make a movie. Maybe you'll have funky little independent movies, and it'll go back and then start up again some other way.

Helen Mirren

The art and science of asking questions is the source of all knowledge.

Thomas Berger

Being good in business is the most fascinating kind of art. Making money is art and working is art and good business is the best art.

Andy Warhol

Mild autism can give you a genius like Einstein. If you have severe autism, you could remain nonverbal. You don't want people to be on the severe end of the spectrum. But if you got rid of all the autism genetics, you wouldn't have science or art. All you would have is a bunch of social 'yak yaks.'

Temple Grandin

The only honest art form is laughter, comedy. You can't fake it... try to fake three laughs in an hour - ha ha ha ha ha - they'll take you away, man. You can't.

Lenny Bruce

We all agree now - by 'we' I mean intelligent people under sixty - that a work of art is like a rose. A rose is not beautiful because it is like something else. Neither is a work of art. Roses and works of art are beautiful in themselves.

Clive Bell

The wonders of the Grand Canyon cannot be adequately represented in symbols of speech, nor by speech itself. The resources of the graphic art are taxed beyond their powers in attempting to portray its features. Language and illustration combined must fail.

John Wesley Powell

The human soul is hungry for beauty; we seek it everywhere -
in landscape, music, art, clothes, furniture, gardening,
companionship, love, religion, and in ourselves. No one would
desire not to be beautiful. When we experience the beautiful,
there is a sense of homecoming.

John O'Donohue

All the art of living lies in a fine mingling of letting go and
holding on.

Havelock Ellis

The art of acceptance is the art of making someone who has
just done you a small favor wish that he might have done you a
greater one.

Martin Luther King, Jr.

Visual art and writing don't exist on an aesthetic hierarchy that
positions one above the other, because each is capable of
things the other can't do at all. Sometimes one picture is equal
to 30 pages of discourse, just as there are things images are
completely incapable of communicating.

William S. Burroughs

The whole art of teaching is only the art of awakening the natural curiosity of young minds for the purpose of satisfying it afterwards.

Anatole France

Patience is the art of hoping.

Luc de Clapiers

To say the word Romanticism is to say modern art - that is, intimacy, spirituality, color, aspiration towards the infinite, expressed by every means available to the arts.

Charles Baudelaire

My focus is my art, and that's what I love to do. I have to be really passionate in order to do something. I've turned down many things that I just didn't believe in.

Beyonce Knowles

If you're not trying to be real, you don't have to get it right. That's art.

Andy Warhol

Telling lies is a fault in a boy, an art in a lover, an accomplishment in a bachelor, and second-nature in a married man.

Helen Rowland

The artist must create a spark before he can make a fire and before art is born, the artist must be ready to be consumed by the fire of his own creation.

Auguste Rodin

I don't listen to what art critics say. I don't know anybody who needs a critic to find out what art is.

Jean-Michel Basquiat

Masterpieces of art possess immense potential to advance a worldview that could help assuage the societal terrors posed by globalization, the most thoroughgoing socioeconomic upheaval since the Industrial Revolution, which has set off a pandemic of retrogressive nationalism, regional separatism, and religious extremism.

Martin Filler

Only in art will the lion lie down with the lamb, and the rose grow without the thorn.

Martin Amis

The art of a people is a true mirror to their minds.

Jawaharlal Nehru

Art is the tree of life. Science is the tree of death.

William Blake

Writing is a kind of performing art, and I can't sit down to write unless I'm dressed. I don't mean dressed in a suit, but dressed well and comfortably and I have to be shaved and bathed.

Peter O'Toole

A lot of country music is sad. I think most art comes out of poverty and hard times. It applies to music. Three chords and the truth - that's what a country song is. There is a lot of heartache in the world.

Willie Nelson

Film editing is now something almost everyone can do at a simple level and enjoy it, but to take it to a higher level requires the same dedication and persistence that any art form does.

Walter Murch

All art is exorcism. I paint dreams and visions too; the dreams and visions of my time. Painting is the effort to produce order; order in yourself. There is much chaos in me, much chaos in our time.

Otto Dix

There is something about giving everything to your profession. In Italian, an obsession is not necessarily negative. It's the art of putting all your energy into one thing; it's the art of transforming even what you eat for lunch into architecture.

Renzo Piano

Once the subject matter of rock n' roll changed from cars and pop love songs to songs about really true love and the blues and death and mortality, this light bulb went off in my head and I went, 'Oh, that's what they're doing. That's kind of - that's art.'

David Chase

Cleanliness is the scourge of art.

Craig Brown

I enjoy going out by myself... always have, always will. I don't have security guards, and, for the most part, I enjoy meeting new people. I see myself as a regular guy who likes playing video games with his nieces and nephews and poker with his family. I don't have an art collection or take exotic vacations. I enjoy being at home.

Vince Vaughn

I've constantly tried new things, even as a child, and have always been obsessed with pink. Now I'm just a little more ladylike and fearless. You should never feel afraid to become a piece of art. It's exhilarating.

Nicki Minaj

Filmmaking, like any other art, is a very profound means of human communication; beyond the professional pleasure of succeeding or the pain of failing, you do want your film to be seen, to communicate itself to other people.

Kenneth Lonergan

All architecture is great architecture after sunset; perhaps architecture is really a nocturnal art, like the art of fireworks.

Gilbert K. Chesterton

We at BMW do not build cars as consumer objects, just to drive from A to B. We build mobile works of art.

Chris Bangle

There are no contests in the Art of Peace. A true warrior is invincible because he or she contests with nothing. Defeat means to defeat the mind of contention that we harbor within.

Morihei Ueshiba

I don't think art is propaganda; it should be something that liberates the soul, provokes the imagination and encourages people to go further. It celebrates humanity instead of manipulating it.

Keith Haring

Comedy is the one absolutely self-aware art form. Actually, hip-hop's another one, I suppose. Because in your songs you're talking about how good a hip-hop artist you are. It's like a painter painting a panting of himself painting a painting.

Bo Burnham

To do a dull thing with style-now that's what I call art.

Charles Bukowski

Education is the art of making man ethical.

Georg Wilhelm Friedrich Hegel

My art is an attempt to reach beyond the surface appearance. I want to see growth in wood, time in stone, nature in a city, and I do not mean its parks but a deeper understanding that a city is nature too-the ground upon which it is built, the stone with which it is made.

Andy Goldsworthy

It is the function of art to renew our perception. What we are familiar with we cease to see. The writer shakes up the familiar scene, and, as if by magic, we see a new meaning in it.

Anais Nin

Art should never be limited - the beauty of art is that it gives us the freedom to go places where we wouldn't go to in our normal lives. Inside, I'm just so many different people. I go from the pretty girl on the red carpet to the singer at Ozzfest, spitting in the crowd. That's Jada.

Jada Pinkett Smith

Our appreciation of folk art will strengthen our identities, our pride in belonging to a community. People trained in the creative use of their hands soon acquire skills, excellent craftsmanship which will be the most important measure of how well we can industrialize.

F. Sionil Jose

The roles of art, morality, religion, political faith, science itself are not to repair organic exhaustion nor to provide sound functioning of the organs. All this supraphysical life is built and expanded not because of the demands of the cosmic environment but because of the demands of the social environment.

Emile Durkheim

Life beats down and crushes the soul and art reminds you that you have one.

Stella Adler

Encouraging young people to believe in themselves and find their own voice whether it's through writing, drama or art is so important in giving young people a sense of self-worth.

Michael Morpurgo

Religion is essentially the art and the theory of the remaking of man. Man is not a finished creation.

Edmund Burke

Regarding race or gender or sexuality, one of the great things about art and music is that they can provide people with very little else in common with a similar entry point for discussion, but the discussions still need to happen for life to get more interesting.

Tunde Adebimpe

There is nothing in the world of art like the songs mother used to sing.

Billy Sunday

Envy is the art of counting the other fellow's blessings instead of your own.

Harold Coffin

To say nothing, especially when speaking, is half the art of diplomacy.

Will Durant

Art is always and everywhere the secret confession, and at the same time the immortal movement of its time.

Karl Marx

Simplicity and repose are the qualities that measure the true value of any work of art.

Frank Lloyd Wright

To catch a husband is an art; to hold him is a job.

Simone de Beauvoir

Where thou art, that is home.

Emily Dickinson

We live in an age when the traditional great subjects - the human form, the landscape, even newer traditions such as abstract expressionism - are daily devalued by commercial art.

Andy Warhol

Music happens to be an art form that transcends language.

Herbie Hancock

Sometimes words are not needed, and the simplicity of expressing yourself through an art form is one of the best ways of communication.

Emmanuel Jal

History repeats itself, but the special call of an art which has passed away is never reproduced. It is as utterly gone out of the world as the song of a destroyed wild bird.

Joseph Conrad

A man's work is nothing but this slow trek to rediscover, through the detours of art, those two or three great and simple images in whose presence his heart first opened.

Albert Camus

Art is making something out of nothing and selling it.

Frank Zappa

Everyone discusses my art and pretends to understand, as if it were necessary to understand, when it is simply necessary to love.

Claude Monet

Men can absent themselves from real life for their art more easily. Women are anchored into the quotidian business of getting food on the table, making sure everybody's socks match, the soccer gear is ready. I admire idealists, but they're usually enabled by someone who holds the tether on their balloon, who pays the bills and sweeps up after them.

Geraldine Brooks

I will never forget experiencing Venice for the first time. It feels like you are transported to another time - the art, music, food and pure romance in the air is like no other place.

Elizabeth Berkley

It is essential to do everything possible to attract young people to opera so they can see that it is not some antiquated art form but a repository of the most glorious music and drama that man has created.

Bruce Beresford

The first 10 years of my professional life had only to do with running away from my father. He was a wonderful cabinet-maker, and me being the eldest son, I had to take over his shop, his profession and so on and so on. I tried to escape by going to art school and then going on to industrial design and then interior design.

Peter Zumthor

The art of storytelling is reaching its end because the epic side of truth, wisdom, is dying out.

Walter Benjamin

I think we're much smarter than we were. Everybody knows that abstract art can be art, and most people know that they may not like it, even if they understand there's another purpose to it.

Roy Lichtenstein

Religion and art spring from the same root and are close kin. Economics and art are strangers.

Nathaniel Hawthorne

So long as the system of competition in the production and exchange of the means of life goes on, the degradation of the arts will go on; and if that system is to last for ever, then art is doomed, and will surely die; that is to say, civilization will die.

William Morris

Art has the power to transform, to illuminate, to educate, inspire and motivate.

Harvey Fierstein

There is no must in art because art is free.

Wassily Kandinsky

Life is the art of being well deceived; and in order that the deception may succeed it must be habitual and uninterrupted.

William Hazlitt

Being a former dancer, classical dancer, it informed me as a human being just in terms of the grace I guess. Ballet is a very graceful form of art. You also become very aware of your body and your mind and your body is working in conjunction. That kind of helps you in acting as well. It's not only using your mind, it's like making your mind communicate this character into your body so that you can bring it to life and physicalize it.

Zoe Saldana

Sculpture is the art of the hole and the lump.

Auguste Rodin

A fool's brain digests philosophy into folly, science into superstition, and art into pedantry. Hence University education.

George Bernard Shaw

I feel like skateboarding is as much of a sport as a lifestyle, and an art form, so there's so much that that transcends in terms of music, fashion, and entertainment.

Tony Hawk

Myth and fairy-story must, as all art, reflect and contain in solution elements of moral and religious truth (or error), but not explicit, not in the known form of the primary 'real' world.

J. R. R. Tolkien

In France, cooking is a serious art form and a national sport.

Julia Child

The art of being wise is the art of knowing what to overlook.

William James

We are all hungry and thirsty for concrete images. Abstract art will have been good for one thing: to restore its exact virginity to figurative art.

Salvador Dali

With just one polka dot, nothing can be achieved. In the universe, there is the sun, the moon, the earth, and hundreds of millions of stars. All of us live in the unfathomable mystery and infinitude of the universe. Pursuing 'philosophy of the universe' through art under such circumstances has led me to what I call 'stereotypical repetition.'

Yayoi Kusama

I think music is the greatest art form that exists, and I think people listen to music for different reasons, and it serves different purposes. Some of it is background music, and some of it is things that might affect a person's day, if not their life, or change an attitude. The best songs are the ones that make you feel something.

Eddie Vedder

Diplomacy: the art of restraining power.

Henry A. Kissinger

Music is your own experience, your own thoughts, your wisdom. If you don't live it, it won't come out of your horn. They teach you there's a boundary line to music. But, man, there's no boundary line to art.

Charlie Parker

Love the art in yourself and not yourself in the art.

Constantin Stanislavski

Freedom of speech is, to all Americans, as oxygen is to the human condition. It is a right that has been irreversibly programmed into our hard drive. We are free to speak our minds. An artist's right to express him or herself as best suits their art, is the artist's prerogative and it is guaranteed.

John C. McGinley

I started to make a study of the art of war and revolution and, whilst abroad, underwent a course in military training. If there was to be guerrilla warfare, I wanted to be able to stand and fight with my people and to share the hazards of war with them.

Nelson Mandela

Growing up going to Christian school and the concept that you're born a sinner and you don't really have a choice to change who you are has been hammered into my head and created the entire reason why I made art and made a band and made records called 'Antichrist Superstar.'

Marilyn Manson

Art is the most beautiful deception of all. And although people try to incorporate the everyday events of life in it, we must hope that it will remain a deception lest it become a utilitarian thing, sad as a factory.

Claude Debussy

The walls between art and engineering exist only in our minds.

Theo Jansen

Democracy is the art and science of running the circus from the monkey cage.

H. L. Mencken

What the mass media offers is not popular art, but entertainment which is intended to be consumed like food, forgotten, and replaced by a new dish.

W. H. Auden

Art is nothing but the expression of our dream; the more we surrender to it the closer we get to the inner truth of things, our dream-life, the true life that scorns questions and does not see them.

Franz Marc

I grew up thinking art was pictures until I got into music and found I was an artist and didn't paint.

Chuck Berry

For art to exist, for any sort of aesthetic activity to exist, a certain physiological precondition is indispensable: intoxication.

Friedrich Nietzsche

In the practical art of war, the best thing of all is to take the enemy's country whole and intact; to shatter and destroy it is not so good.

Sun Tzu

Censorship is to art as lynching is to justice.

Henry Louis Gates

I'd love to go to art school. I'd love to learn how to draw. I'd love to be fluent in Spanish. I'd like to be a brain surgeon.

Billie Joe Armstrong

'Untitled' is a time machine that can transport you to 1992, an edgy moment when the art world was crumbling, money was scarce, and artists like Tiravanija were in the nascent stages of combining Happenings, performance art, John Cage, Joseph Beuys, and the do-it-yourself ethos of punk. Meanwhile, a new art world was coming into being.

Jerry Saltz

Bullfighting is the only art in which the artist is in danger of death and in which the degree of brilliance in the performance is left to the fighter's honor.

Ernest Hemingway

The art of motherhood involves much silent, unobtrusive self-denial, an hourly devotion which finds no detail too minute.

Honore de Balzac

Good art provides people with a vocabulary about things they can't articulate.

Mos Def

The strangeness will wear off and I think we will discover the deeper meanings in modern art.

Jackson Pollock

Art is nothing if you don't reach every segment of the people.

Keith Haring

My life is a monument to procrastination, to the art of putting things off until later, or much later, or possibly never.

Craig Brown

We were astonished by the beauty and refinement of the art displayed by the objects surpassing all we could have imagined - the impression was overwhelming.

Howard Carter

Ballet is an incredibly difficult, beautiful art form that takes a lot of training, a lot of time, and a lot of hard work.

Sutton Foster

The foundation of empire is art and science. Remove them or degrade them, and the empire is no more. Empire follows art and not vice versa as Englishmen suppose.

William Blake

Patience is the art of concealing your impatience.

Guy Kawasaki

A good mother remembers to serve fruit at breakfast, is always cheerful and never yells, manages not to project her own neuroses and inadequacies onto her children, is an active and beloved community volunteer. She remembers to make play dates, her children's clothes fit, she does art projects with them and enjoys all their games.

Ayelet Waldman

When thou art at Rome, do as they do at Rome.

Miguel de Cervantes

Madness is the absolute break with the work of art; it forms the constitutive moment of abolition, which dissolves in time the truth of the work of art.

Michel Foucault

Death is an endless night so awful to contemplate that it can make us love life and value it with such passion that it may be the ultimate cause of all joy and all art.

Paul Theroux

Art is for everybody.

Keith Haring

If you go back to the Greeks and Romans, they talk about all three - wine, food, and art - as a way of enhancing life.

Robert Mondavi

When I was a freshman in high school, I read a book about the making of Disney's 'Sleeping Beauty' called 'The Art of Animation.' It was this weird revelation for me, because I hadn't considered that people actually get paid to make cartoons.

John Lasseter

I went into the business for the money, and the art grew out of it. If people are disillusioned by that remark, I can't help it. It's the truth.

Charlie Chaplin

There are worlds of experience beyond the world of the aggressive man, beyond history, and beyond science. The moods and qualities of nature and the revelations of great art are equally difficult to define; we can grasp them only in the depths of our perceptive spirit.

Ansel Adams

The art of effective listening is essential to clear communication, and clear communication is necessary to management success.

James Cash Penney

Interpretation is the revenge of the intellectual upon art.

Susan Sontag

I try to keep a low profile in general. Not with my art, but just as a person.

Alanis Morissette

You can be good at technology and like fashion and art. You can be good at technology and be a jock. You can be good at technology and be a mom. You can do it your way, on your terms.

Marissa Mayer

The public history of modern art is the story of conventional people not knowing what they are dealing with.

Golda Meir

A painter, who finds no satisfaction in mere representation, however artistic, in his longing to express his inner life, cannot but envy the ease with which music, the most non-material of the arts today, achieves this end. He naturally seeks to apply the methods of music to his own art.

Wassily Kandinsky

Although my art work was heavily informed by my design work on a formal and visual level, as regards meaning and content the two practices parted ways.

Barbara Kruger

Art is the elimination of the unnecessary.

Pablo Picasso

All great art is the work of the whole living creature, body and soul, and chiefly of the soul.

John Ruskin

To speak of morals in art is to speak of legislature in sex. Art is the sex of the imagination.

George Jean Nathan

Art to me is an anecdote of the spirit, and the only means of making concrete the purpose of its varied quickness and stillness.

Mark Rothko

I love photography, and I love the art of photography.

Helen Mirren

Postmodernism surely requires an even greater grasp of symbolism, as it's increasingly an art of gesture alone.

Andrew Eldritch

To my mind the old masters are not art; their value is in their scarcity.

Thomas A. Edison

The art of mastering life is the prerequisite for all further forms of expression, whether they are paintings, sculptures, tragedies, or musical compositions.

Paul Klee

I've always enjoyed feeling a connection to the avant-garde, such as Dada and surrealism and pop art. The only thing the artist can do is be honest with themselves and make the art they want to make. That's what I've always done.

Jeff Koons

Art is a lie that makes us realize truth.

Pablo Picasso

In India, music is not given its due. Music is still treated as a hobby. Art does not have that recognition, be it music, writing, literature or sports. In the West, a famed singer or Hollywood actor generates equal respect and weightage as compared to a scientist. But science, engineering or M.B.A. are still the most sought after professions here.

Kailash Kher

The art of life is to live in the present moment, and to make that moment as perfect as we can by the realization that we are the instruments and expression of God Himself.

Emmet Fox

Like art, revolutions come from combining what exists into what has never existed before.

Gloria Steinem

We can learn the art of fierce compassion - redefining strength, deconstructing isolation and renewing a sense of community, practicing letting go of rigid us-vs.-them thinking - while cultivating power and clarity in response to difficult situations.

Sharon Salzberg

Sculpture is the art of the intelligence.

Pablo Picasso

The screen is a magic medium. It has such power that it can retain interest as it conveys emotions and moods that no other art form can hope to tackle.

Stanley Kubrick

Life is the art of drawing sufficient conclusions from insufficient premises.

Samuel Butler

Modesty: the gentle art of enhancing your charm by pretending not to be aware of it.

Oliver Herford

Cunning is the art of concealing our own defects, and discovering other people's weaknesses.

William Hazlitt

Art is built on the deepest themes of human meaning: good and evil, beauty and ugliness, life and death, love and hate. No other story has incarnated those themes more than the story of Jesus.

John Ortberg

Speaking for myself, art differs from writing in that I never know what I'm going to paint until I paint it, so it's almost like automatic writing. A writer, on the other hand, can't help but know what he's going to write, because the activity demands a degree of premeditation.

William S. Burroughs

For me, pointing and clicking my phone is absolutely fine. People say that isn't the art of photography but I don't agree.

Annie Lennox

If Art relates itself to an Object, it becomes descriptive, divisionist, literary.

Robert Delaunay

Memory is a great artist. For every man and for every woman it makes the recollection of his or her life a work of art and an unfaithful record.

Andre Maurois

What strikes me is the fact that in our society, art has become something which is only related to objects, and not to individuals, or to life.

Michel Foucault

Great art is the outward expression of an inner life in the artist, and this inner life will result in his personal vision of the world.

Edward Hopper

I have discovered the art of deceiving diplomats. I tell them the truth and they never believe me.

Camillo di Cavour

Architecture is basically the design of interiors, the art of organizing interior space.

Philip Johnson

The show business has all phases and grades of dignity, from the exhibition of a monkey to the exposition of that highest art in music or the drama which secures for the gifted artists a world-wide fame princes well might envy.

P. T. Barnum

I believe love at first sight is possible. Centuries of literature and art and beauty has been dedicated to that idea, so who am I to argue, even if I've never experienced it?

Maggie Grace

And since geometry is the right foundation of all painting, I have decided to teach its rudiments and principles to all youngsters eager for art.

Albrecht Durer

To injure an opponent is to injure yourself. To control aggression without inflicting injury is the Art of Peace.

Morihei Ueshiba

I say that democracy can never prove itself beyond cavil, until it founds and luxuriantly grows its own forms of art, poems, schools, theology, displacing all that exists, or that has been produced anywhere in the past, under opposite influences.

Walt Whitman

There is in fact no such thing as art for art's sake, art that stands above classes, art that is detached from or independent of politics. Proletarian literature and art are part of the whole proletarian revolutionary cause.

Mao Zedong

I don't believe in the school of hard knocks, although I've had them. All that stuff about whatever doesn't kill you makes you stronger is so not true. Do you know what makes you stronger? When people treat you and your art with dignity.

Lana Del Rey

People think that computer science is the art of geniuses but the actual reality is the opposite, just many people doing things that build on eachother, like a wall of mini stones.

Donald Knuth

Look. Art knows no prejudice, art knows no boundaries, art doesn't really have judgement in it's purest form. So just go, just go.

K. D. Lang

Life is an illusion. I am held together in the nothingness by art.

Anselm Kiefer

It is through art, and through art only, that we can realise our perfection.

Oscar Wilde

The most seductive thing about art is the personality of the artist himself.

Paul Cezanne

Does art have a future? Performance genres like opera, theater, music and dance are thriving all over the world, but the visual arts have been in slow decline for nearly 40 years. No major figure of profound influence has emerged in painting or sculpture since the waning of Pop Art and the birth of Minimalism in the early 1970s.

Camille Paglia

Creative output, you know, is just pain. I'm going to be cliche for a minute and say that great art comes from pain.

Kanye West

What other people may find in poetry or art museums, I find in the flight of a good drive.

Arnold Palmer

Art is a way to express yourself and through that you can escape a bad situation.

Russell Simmons

Writing stopped being fun when I discovered the difference between good writing and bad and, even more terrifying, the difference between it and true art. And after that, the whip came down.

Truman Capote

Madonna remains the most visible performer on the planet, as well as one of the wealthiest, but would anyone seriously say that artistic self-development is her primary motivating principle? She is too busy with Kabbalah, fashion merchandising, adoption melodramas, the gym, and ill-starred horseback riding to study art.

Camille Paglia

Art is elemental. Reason alone as it's expressed in the sciences can't be man's complete answer to reality, and it can't express everything that man can, wants to, and has to express. I think God built this into man. Art along with science is the highest gift God has given him.

Pope Benedict XVI

To create a work of art is to create the world.

Wassily Kandinsky

As a composer and as a musician I'm a true believer - and this is not to be overly diplomatic - I'm a believer that there's artistry in everything from a lawn gnome to a desk chair to a symphony to an Andy Warhol painting. There's art in absolutely everything.

Darren Criss

Sometimes being a friend means mastering the art of timing. There is a time for silence. A time to let go and allow people to hurl themselves into their own destiny. And a time to prepare to pick up the pieces when it's all over.

Octavia E. Butler

Art raises its head where creeds relax.

Friedrich Nietzsche

We all know that Art is not truth. Art is a lie that makes us realize the truth, at least the truth that is given to us to understand.

Pablo Picasso

I paint; I draw and paint - I've been doing that since I was in third grade, drawing realistically and then changing to abstract art. That was my first creative thing before guitar or comedy.

Steven Wright

Art is the objectification of feeling.

Herman Melville

An art which isn't based on feeling isn't an art at all.

Paul Cezanne

Great artists are people who find the way to be themselves in their art. Any sort of pretension induces mediocrity in art and life alike.

Margot Fonteyn

Skill without imagination is craftsmanship and gives us many useful objects such as wickerwork picnic baskets. Imagination without skill gives us modern art.

Tom Stoppard

We have been so successful in the past century at the art of living longer and staying alive that we have forgotten how to die. Too often we learn the hard way. As soon as the baby boomers pass pensionable age, their lesson will be harsher still.

Terry Pratchett

Modernity is the transient, the fleeting, the contingent; it is one half of art, the other being the eternal and the immovable.

Charles Baudelaire

Football is an art, like dancing is an art - but only when it's well done does it become an art.

Arsene Wenger

There are no rules. That is how art is born, how breakthroughs happen. Go against the rules or ignore the rules. That is what invention is about.

Helen Frankenthaler

The art of letters will come to an end before A.D. 2000. I shall survive as a curiosity.

Ezra Pound

We should always remember that sensitiveness and emotion constitute the real content of a work of art.

Maurice Ravel

Architecture is art, nothing else.

Philip Johnson

There is hardly any money interest in art, and music will be there when money is gone.

Duke Ellington

Imagine it's 1981. You're an artist, in love with art, smitten with art history. You're also a woman, with almost no mentors to look to; art history just isn't that into you. Any woman approaching art history in the early eighties was attempting to enter an almost foreign country, a restricted and exclusionary domain that spoke a private language.

Jerry Saltz

I mean, making art is about objectifying your experience of the world, transforming the flow of moments into something visual, or textual, or musical, whatever. Art creates a kind of commentary.

Barbara Kruger

If commercialization is putting my art on a shirt so that a kid who can't afford a $30,000 painting can buy one, then I'm all for it.

Keith Haring

My art originates from hallucinations only I can see. I translate the hallucinations and obsessional images that plague me into sculptures and paintings.

Yayoi Kusama

In art, at a certain level, there is no 'better than.' It's just about trying to operate for yourself on the most supreme level, artistically, that you can and hoping that people get it. Trusting that, just because of the way people are built and how interconnected we are, greatness will translate and symmetry will be recognised.

Frank Ocean

Melbourne, where I grew up, is one of the street art capitals of the world. Something about discovering freshly painted walls always fills me with optimism; it's autonomous and democratic, and reminds me that maybe people are paying attention after all.

Penelope Mitchell

When you create art, the world has to wait.

Will Smith

The greatness of art is not to find what is common but what is unique.

Isaac Bashevis Singer

Art! Who comprehends her? With whom can one consult concerning this great goddess?

Ludwig van Beethoven

Simplicity is the final achievement. After one has played a vast quantity of notes and more notes, it is simplicity that emerges as the crowning reward of art.

Frederic Chopin

Everything a writer learns about the art or craft of fiction takes just a little away from his need or desire to write at all. In the end he knows all the tricks and has nothing to say.

Raymond Chandler

Any form of art is a form of power; it has impact, it can affect change - it can not only move us, it makes us move.

Ossie Davis

Actually I think Art lies in both directions - the broad strokes, big picture but on the other hand the minute examination of the apparently mundane. Seeing the whole world in a grain of sand, that kind of thing.

Peter Hammill

No art is less spontaneous than mine. What I do is the result of reflection and the study of the great masters.

Edgar Degas

I think all art is about control - the encounter between control and the uncontrollable.

Richard Avedon

You can go to Graff and buy a diamond that's flawless. You aren't going to be able to buy the same diamond at Fortunoff, but it's still a diamond you can enjoy. If fashion can allow you to have the Chanel mystique through a lipstick, then why shouldn't art allow you to have that through a sweatshirt that says 'Cremaster' on it?

Marc Jacobs

During the Middle Ages they understood that words accompanied by imagery are much more memorable. By making the margins of a book colorful and beautiful, illuminations help make the text unforgettable. It's unfortunate that we've lost the art of illumination.

Joshua Foer

Great art - or good art - is when you look at it, experience it and it stays in your mind. I don't think conceptual art and traditional art are all that different.

Damien Hirst

Supreme serenity still remains the Ideal of great Art. The shapes and transitory forms of life are but stages toward this Ideal, which Christ's religion illuminates with His divine light.

Franz Liszt

What a museum chooses to exhibit is sometimes less important than how such decisions are made and what values inform them. To have the crucial role of museum professionals usurped by self-serving tycoons in the name of economic imperative threatens not only the integrity of individual institutions but the very principle of art held in public trust.

Martin Filler

By 3000 B.C. the art of Egypt was so ripe and so far advanced that it is surprising to find any student of early culture proposing that the crude contemporary art of the early Babylonians is the product of a civilization earlier than that of the Nile.

James Henry Breasted

Besides the noble art of getting things done, there is the noble art of leaving things undone. The wisdom of life consists in the elimination of non-essentials.

Lin Yutang

Life is the only art that we are required to practice without preparation, and without being allowed the preliminary trials, the failures and botches, that are essential for training.

Lewis Mumford

Dance is the only art of which we ourselves are the stuff of which it is made.

Ted Shawn

Insurrection is an art, and like all arts has its own laws.

Leon Trotsky

Too often, complaint is not about principled objection on moral grounds, but opportunistic objection on grounds of self-interest. To rectify this, we need to work on mastering the art of complaint.

Julian Baggini

Life is a lot more interesting if you are interested in the people and the places around you. So, illuminate your little patch of ground, the people that you know, the things that you want to commemorate. Light them up with your art, with your music, with your writing, with whatever it is that you do.

Alan Moore

Art is not for the cultivated taste. It is to cultivate taste.

Nikki Giovanni

What goes on in abstract art is the proclaiming of aesthetic principles... It is in our own time that we have become aware of pure aesthetic considerations. Art never can be imitation.

Hans Hofmann

I don't like to say I have given my life to art. I prefer to say art has given me my life.

Frank Stella

I do not deny that I have made drawings and watercolors of an erotic nature. But they are always works of art. Are there no artists who have done erotic pictures?

Egon Schiele

No nude, however abstract, should fail to arouse in the spectator some vestige of erotic feeling, even if it be only the faintest shadow - and if it does not do so it is bad art and false morals.

Kenneth Clark

Even though you can't expect to defeat the absurdity of the world, you must make the attempt. That's morality, that's religion, that's art, that's life.

Phil Ochs

Art led the way for me to recover. He got out of prison before me and started traveling all over the world before I did. He showed me by example that it could be done, and I'll always love him for that.

Frank Morgan

I go into any movie that's historical fiction thinking, 'OK, I'm here to watch a work of art, something delivering a series of opinions, and if it's a good work of art, these opinions become so deeply embedded in complexity and richness that I won't even be bothered by the opinions. I'll make my own mind up.'

Tony Kushner

Truly fertile Music, the only kind that will move us, that we shall truly appreciate, will be a Music conducive to Dream, which banishes all reason and analysis. One must not wish first to understand and then to feel. Art does not tolerate Reason.

Albert Camus

Music is the art of the prophets and the gift of God.

Martin Luther

I believe entertainment can aspire to be art, and can become art, but if you set out to make art you're an idiot.

Steve Martin

I see no reason why the artistic world can't absolutely merge with Madison Avenue. Pop art is a move in that direction. Why can't we have advertisements with beautiful words and beautiful images?

William S. Burroughs

African art is functional, it serves a purpose. It's not a dormant. It's not a means to collect the largest cheering section. It should be healing, a source a joy. Spreading positive vibrations.

Mos Def

The goal of art was the vital expression of self.

Alfred Stieglitz

Literature is the art of writing something that will be read twice; journalism what will be grasped at once.

Cyril Connolly

Of all the seasons, winter is the most conducive to the great art of dormancy. This art requires an appreciation of semi-consciousness: the beautiful and necessary prelude to sleep - a special pleasure in itself that is all too often neglected, under-valued or looked down upon.

Michael Leunig

Female artists are the perfect example of a creator: They know how to make life and art with their bodies. Life comes from their bodies, so on a very basic level, they have more to write about.

Brandon Boyd

Art is eternal, but life is short.

Evelyn de Morgan

The beautiful is in nature, and it is encountered under the most diverse forms of reality. Once it is found it belongs to art, or rather to the artist who discovers it.

Gustave Courbet

I think there's escapist moviemaking, and we want to be captivated and taken away. If it's done right, you can craft an incredible film. There have been superhero films that I think are brilliant pieces of art.

Ryan Reynolds

I think TV promulgates the idea that good art is just art which makes people like and depend on the vehicle that brings them the art.

David Foster Wallace

Art hath an enemy called Ignorance.

Ben Jonson

I used language because I wanted to offer content that people - not necessarily art people - could understand.

Jenny Holzer

There's an axiom I live by: 'There is no art without politics.' You either choose to engage it, or you choose political apathy. This ties in with ideas around real-time performance and feedback.

Chris Jordan

If you practice an art, be proud of it and make it proud of you It may break your heart, but it will fill your heart before it breaks it; it will make you a person in your own right.

Maxwell Anderson

You don't have to have a great art idea - just get to work and something will happen. So that's pretty much my modus operandi and pretty much my principal position, such as it is.

Chuck Close

For when it is the good that is under consideration, and the ethical object is predominant, truth must be considered more in reference to art than science, if, that is, unity is to be preserved in the work generally.

Friedrich Schleiermacher

I like writing letters and receiving letters. It's a shame that we've lost the art of letter-writing and saving correspondence. I mourn that.

Elizabeth McGovern

Art is not predictable. Art is not golf, as great as that may be. There are 360 degrees of choice to make.

Tina Weymouth

Poetry is an art, and chief of the fine art; the easiest to dabble in, the hardest in which to reach true excellence.

Edmund Clarence Stedman

The best advice on the art of being happy is about as easy to follow as advice to be well when one is sick.

Sophie Swetchine

I think making a movie is like drawing or creating an art piece. The artwork reflects part of your personality, but not all.

Tony Jaa

The real art of conducting consists in transitions.

Gustav Mahler

The art of living does not consist in preserving and clinging to a particular mode of happiness, but in allowing happiness to change its form without being disappointed by the change; happiness, like a child, must be allowed to grow up.

Charles Morgan

You should never feel afraid to become a piece of art. It's exhilarating.

Nicki Minaj

Courtesy is a silver lining around the dark clouds of civilization; it is the best part of refinement and in many ways, an art of heroic beauty in the vast gallery of man's cruelty and baseness.

Bryant H. McGill

All things are artificial, for nature is the art of God.

Thomas Browne

I wash my hands of those who imagine chattering to be knowledge, silence to be ignorance, and affection to be art.

Khalil Gibran

Religion is the masterpiece of the art of animal training, for it trains people as to how they shall think.

Arthur Schopenhauer

My philosophy is that I'm an artist. I perform an art not with a paint brush or a camera. I perform with bodily movement. Instead of exhibiting my art in a museum or a book or on canvas, I exhibit my art in front of the multitudes.

Steve Prefontaine

Politics is the art of controlling your environment.

Hunter S. Thompson

Some people have been kind enough to call me a fine artist. I've always called myself an illustrator. I'm not sure what the difference is. All I know is that whatever type of work I do, I try to give it my very best. Art has been my life.

Norman Rockwell

Diplomacy is the art of saying 'Nice doggie' until you can find a rock.

Will Rogers

One does not need buildings, money, power, or status to practice the Art of Peace. Heaven is right where you are standing, and that is the place to train.

Morihei Ueshiba

Good manners is the art of making those people easy with whom we converse. Whoever makes the fewest people uneasy is the best bred in the room.

Jonathan Swift

I am my own experiment. I am my own work of art.

Madonna Ciccone

The art challenges the technology, and the technology inspires the art.

John Lasseter

There will be very few occasions when you are absolutely certain about anything. You will consistently be called upon to make decisions with limited information. That being the case, your goal should not be to eliminate uncertainty. Instead, you must develop the art of being clear in the face of uncertainty.

Andy Stanley

In our fast-forward culture, we have lost the art of eating well. Food is often little more than fuel to pour down the hatch while doing other stuff - surfing the Web, driving, walking along the street. Dining al desko is now the norm in many workplaces. All of this speed takes a toll. Obesity, eating disorders and poor nutrition are rife.

Carl Honore

The great art of life is sensation, to feel that we exist, even in pain.

Lord Byron

And the first rude sketch that the world had seen was joy to his mighty heart, till the Devil whispered behind the leaves 'It's pretty, but is it Art?'

Rudyard Kipling

I don't think about art when I'm working. I try to think about
life.

Jean-Michel Basquiat

I adore art... when I am alone with my notes, my heart pounds
and the tears stream from my eyes, and my emotion and my
joys are too much to bear.

Giuseppe Verdi

Art is longing. You never arrive, but you keep going in the
hope that you will.

Anselm Kiefer

In the big picture, architecture is the art and science of making
sure that our cities and buildings fit with the way we want to
live our lives.

Bjarke Ingels

I believe the target of anything in life should be to do it so well
that it becomes an art.

Arsene Wenger

The way I make art - the way a lot of people make art - is as an extension of language and communication, where references are incredibly important.

Shepard Fairey

The art of leadership is saying no, not saying yes. It is very easy to say yes.

Tony Blair

Muhammad Ali - he was a magnificent fighter and he was an icon... Every head must bow, every knee must bend, every tongue must confess, thou art the greatest, the greatest of all time, Muhammad, Muhammad Ali.

Don King

Yes, the Bible should be taught in our schools because it is necessary to understand the Bible if we are to truly understand our own culture and how it came to be. The Bible has influenced every part of western culture from our art, music, and history, to our sense of fairness, charity, and business.

Joel Osteen

He who would do good to another must do it in Minute Particulars: general Good is the plea of the scoundrel, hypocrite, and flatterer, for Art and Science cannot exist but in minutely organized Particulars.

William Blake

A work of art which did not begin in emotion is not art.

Paul Cezanne

There is nothing new in art except talent.

Anton Chekhov

The excellency of every art is its intensity, capable of making all disagreeable evaporate.

John Keats

Like music and art, love of nature is a common language that can transcend political or social boundaries.

Jimmy Carter

Raising children is a creative endeavor, an art rather than a science.

Bruno Bettelheim

Why must art be static? You look at an abstraction, sculptured or painted, an entirely exciting arrangement of planes, spheres, nuclei, entirely without meaning. It would be perfect, but it is always still. The next step in sculpture is motion.

Alexander Calder

The aim of all commentary on art now should be to make works of art - and, by analogy, our own experience - more, rather than less, real to us. The function of criticism should be to show how it is what it is, even that it is what it is, rather than to show what it means.

Susan Sontag

So then learn to conquer your fear. This is the only art we have to master nowadays: to look at things without fear, and to fearlessly do right.

Friedrich Durrenmatt

I think of horror films as art, as films of confrontation. Films that make you confront aspects of your own life that are difficult to face. Just because you're making a horror film doesn't mean you can't make an artful film.

David Cronenberg

Where the spirit does not work with the hand, there is no art.

Leonardo da Vinci

Art washes away from the soul the dust of everyday life.

Pablo Picasso

Every happening, great and small, is a parable whereby God speaks to us, and the art of life is to get the message.

Malcolm Muggeridge

Ethics is in origin the art of recommending to others the sacrifices required for cooperation with oneself.

Bertrand Russell

Life doesn't imitate art, it imitates bad television.

Woody Allen

In life, as in art, the beautiful moves in curves.

Edward G. Bulwer-Lytton

The educator must believe in the potential power of his pupil, and he must employ all his art in seeking to bring his pupil to experience this power.

Alfred Adler

I am not a great cook, I am not a great artist, but I love art, and I love food, so I am the perfect traveller.

Michael Palin

We haven't lost romance in the digital age, but we may be neglecting it. In doing so, antiquated art forms are taking on new importance. The power of a handwritten letter is greater than ever. It's personal and deliberate and means more than an e-mail or text ever will.

Ashton Kutcher

I'm inspired by artists and musicians. There are so many wonderful and talented people in the world. I love discovering new music, new writers, or new art.

Alicia Keys

Art, whatever form it takes, requires hard work, craftsmanship and creativity. As a writer, I know my grammar, cadence, the music of prose, and the art of the narrative.

F. Sionil Jose

Society is like a large piece of frozen water; and skating well is the great art of social life.

Letitia Elizabeth Landon

Because it's so easy to medicate our need for self-worth by pandering to win followers, 'likes' and view counts, social media have become the metier of choice for many people who might otherwise channel that energy into books, music or art - or even into their own Web ventures.

Neil Strauss

It is only an auctioneer who can equally and impartially admire all schools of art.

Oscar Wilde

A work of art is above all an adventure of the mind.

Eugene Ionesco

Winners have the ability to step back from the canvas of their lives like an artist gaining perspective. They make their lives a work of art - an individual masterpiece.

Denis Waitley

Gossip is the art of saying nothing in a way that leaves practically nothing unsaid.

Walter Winchell

Art can never exist without naked beauty displayed.

William Blake

Irresponsibility is part of the pleasure of all art; it is the part the schools cannot recognize.

James Joyce

Really I don't like human nature unless all candied over with art.

Virginia Woolf

Every human is an artist. And this is the main art that we have: the creation of our story.

Miguel Angel Ruiz

We work in the dark - we do what we can - we give what we have. Our doubt is our passion and our passion is our task. The rest is the madness of art.

Henry James

History has remembered the kings and warriors, because they destroyed; art has remembered the people, because they created.

William Morris

In science, if you don't do it, somebody else will. Whereas in art, if Beethoven didn't compose the 'Ninth Symphony,' no one else before or after is going to compose the 'Ninth Symphony' that he composed; no one else is going to paint 'Starry Night' by van Gogh.

Neil deGrasse Tyson

The concept of commercialism in the fashion and art world is looked down upon. You know, just to think, 'What amount of creativity does it take to make something that masses of people like?' And, 'How does creativity apply across the board?'

Kanye West

Art is the imposing of a pattern on experience, and our aesthetic enjoyment is recognition of the pattern.

Alfred North Whitehead

Self-censorship is a lie to yourself; if you are going to be trying to seriously create art, to create literary art, and you decide to hold back, to censor yourself, then you are a fool to yourself and it would be better that you kept your mouth shut and did not speak.

Salman Rushdie

I'm not really sure what social message my art carries, if any. And I don't really want it to carry one. I'm not interested in the subject matter to try to teach society anything, or to try to better our world in any way.

Roy Lichtenstein

President Obama called for a 'we' nation in his Inauguration Address. Art convenes. It is not just inspirational. It is aspirational. It pricks the walls of our compartmentalized minds, opens our hearts and makes us brave. And that's what we need most in our country today.

Anna Deavere Smith

Nothing is art if it does not come from nature.

Antoni Gaudi

For me, visuals are as important as the music. I just love escapism and giving people something to escape to. To me, that's what art is.

Iggy Azalea

When you walk down the street and see something in a crazy spot, there's something powerful about that. The street will always be an important part of getting art out there for me.

Shepard Fairey

Life imitates art far more than art imitates Life.

Oscar Wilde

The moment you think you understand a great work of art, it's dead for you.

Oscar Wilde

What we have to do, what at any rate it is our duty to do, is to revive the old art of Lying.

Oscar Wilde

I do not know what the spirit of a philosopher could more wish to be than a good dancer. For the dance is his ideal, also his fine art, finally also the only kind of piety he knows, his 'divine service.'

Friedrich Nietzsche

A beautiful body perishes, but a work of art dies not.

Leonardo da Vinci

My art is not limited to the songs I create but also to the reaction it creates. I like to sit back and look at the whole thing as if it's a tornado that I'm controlling. It's creating chaos. When you create chaos, ideas are turned upside down, and everybody looks at things in a different way.

Marilyn Manson

If you cannot learn to love real art, at least learn to hate sham art and reject it.

William Morris

If a patron buys from an artist who needs money, the patron then makes himself equal to the artist; he is building art into the world; he creates.

Ezra Pound

Picasso said, 'Art is a lie that tells the truth.' What if you just want to tell the truth and not lie about it?

Nicolas Cage

Art is made to disturb, science reassures.

Georges Braque

If a man devotes himself to art, much evil is avoided that happens otherwise if one is idle.

Albrecht Durer

All equestrians, if they last long enough, learn that riding in whatever form is a lifelong sport and art, an endeavor that is both familiar and new every time you take the horse out of his stall or pasture.

Jane Smiley

Anyone who works on a quilt, who devotes her time, energy, creativity, and passion to that art, learns to value the work of her hands. And as any quilter will tell you, a quilter's quilting friends are some of the dearest, most generous, and most supportive people she knows.

Jennifer Chiaverini

Art attracts us only by what it reveals of our most secret self.

Jean-Luc Godard

Pitching is the art of instilling fear.

Sandy Koufax

The house has to please everyone, contrary to the work of art which does not. The work is a private matter for the artist. The house is not.

Adolf Loos

My own interest in art was because of my mother. My father didn't like contemporary art, so he didn't give her large sums to spend. So, she began buying prints and drawings. During my school days, I remember sitting in on many of the early meetings.

David Rockefeller

I was taught that to create anything you had to believe in failure, simply because you had to be prepared to go through an idea without any fear. Failure, you learned, as I did in art school, to be a wonderful thing. It allowed you to get up in the morning and take the pillow off your head.

Malcolm Mclaren

Art is, for me, the process of trying to wake up the soul. Because we live in an industrialized, fast-paced world that prefers that the soul remain asleep.

Bill Viola

Architecture is a art when one consciously or unconsciously creates aesthetic emotion in the atmosphere and when this environment produces well being.

Luis Barragan

If you're a new artist, practice your art and share it. Set up shop somewhere, whether it's a street corner or a coffee shop. I got my start in a coffee shop that didn't even have live music. I wanted to play in coffee shops that did have live music, but I didn't have an audience.

Jason Mraz

If my art has nothing to do with people's pain and sorrow, what is 'art' for?

Ai Weiwei

Does it follow that the house has nothing in common with art and is architecture not to be included in the arts? Only a very small part of architecture belongs to art: the tomb and the monument. Everything else that fulfils a function is to be excluded from the domain of art.

Adolf Loos

The most powerful words in English are 'Tell me a story,' words that are intimately related to the complexity of history, the origins of language, the continuity of the species, the taproot of our humanity, our singularity, and art itself.

Pat Conroy

Admiration for a quality or an art can be so strong that it deters us from striving to possess it.

Friedrich Nietzsche

If being an egomaniac means I believe in what I do and in my art or music, then in that respect you can call me that... I believe in what I do, and I'll say it.

John Lennon

The person who knows one thing and does it better than anyone else, even if it only be the art of raising lentils, receives the crown he merits. If he raises all his energy to that end, he is a benefactor of mankind and its rewarded as such.

Og Mandino

We're going to shoot one Polaroid per show. I'm going to sign this before it even develops because I know that once it develops with my signature on it, it's worth a fortune. I'll make this a work of magic warlock art.

Charlie Sheen

It's clever, but is it Art?

Rudyard Kipling

Art does not reproduce what we see; rather, it makes us see.

Paul Klee

The art of pleasing is the art of deception.

Luc de Clapiers

Don't be an art critic. Paint. There lies salvation.

Paul Cezanne

Words may be false and full of art; Sighs are the natural language of the heart.

Thomas Shadwell

In the first book of my Discworld series, published more than 26 years ago, I introduced Death as a character; there was nothing particularly new about this - death has featured in art and literature since medieval times, and for centuries we have had a fascination with the Grim Reaper.

Terry Pratchett

Art cannot be modern. Art is primordially eternal.

Egon Schiele

All art is a struggle to be, in a particular sort of way, virtuous.

Iris Murdoch

Becoming emancipated at 14, my life wasn't normal. I didn't have to go to school, so I didn't. I was rebellious by nature. I spent my 20s focusing on my company, Flower Films, and producing movies. Now that I'm almost 30, I would like to try other things in lie. I'm crazy about photography, and I want to take an art history class.

Drew Barrymore

The body is your instrument in dance, but your art is outside that creature, the body.

Martha Graham

When lovely woman stoops to folly, and finds too late that men betray, what charm can soothe her melancholy, what art can wash her guilt away?

Oliver Goldsmith

Translation is the art of failure.

Umberto Eco

I did study the art of being a barber because I wanted to figure out what my routine would be. Do you start in the front or back? Top or bottom? Swivel the chair or walk around? What I did discover is there's no such thing as the perfect haircut!

Sean Patrick Thomas

I like to change. A new lamp, a piece of art, can transform a room.

Madonna Ciccone

You've got to invest in the world, you've got to read, you've got to go to art galleries, you've got to find out the names of plants. You've got to start to love the world and know about the whole genius of the human race. We're amazing people.

Vivienne Westwood

When hospitality becomes an art it loses its very soul.

Max Beerbohm

For me, there is very little difference between magic and art. To me, the ultimate act of magic is to create something from nothing: It's like when the stage magician pulls the rabbit from the hat.

Alan Moore

The great art of films does not consist of descriptive movement of face and body but in the movements of thought and soul transmitted in a kind of intense isolation.

Louise Brooks

Wisdom is nothing but a preparation of the soul, a capacity, a secret art of thinking, feeling and breathing thoughts of unity at every moment of life.

Herman Hesse

All of Koons's best art - the encased vacuum cleaners, the stainless-steel Rabbit (the late-twentieth century's signature work of Simulationist sculpture), the amazing gleaming Balloon Dog, and the cast-iron re-creation of a Civil War mortar exhibited last month at the Armory - has simultaneously flaunted extreme realism, idealism, and fantasy.

Jerry Saltz

One must do the same subject over again ten times, a hundred times. In art nothing must resemble an accident, not even movement.

Edgar Degas

All art constantly aspires towards the condition of music.

Walter Pater

Fortunately art is a community effort - a small but select community living in a spiritualized world endeavoring to interpret the wars and the solitudes of the flesh.

Allen Ginsberg

Art is the provocation for talking about enigma and the search for sense in human life. One can do that by telling a story or writing about a fresco by Giotto or studying how a snail climbs up a wall.

John Berger

The great thing that guys like Facebook's Mark Zuckerberg and the Google guys have in common is they treat their technology like it's art, and I suppose in the hands of virtuosos like them, it is.

Harvey Weinstein

Dancers are a work of art - they are the canvas on which their work is painted.

Patrick Duffy

Art's a very metaphysical activity. It's something that enriches the parameters of your life, the possibilities of being, and you touch transcendence and you change your life. And you want to change the life of others, too. That's why people are involved with art.

Jeff Koons

If Antarctica were music it would be Mozart. Art, and it would be Michelangelo. Literature, and it would be Shakespeare. And yet it is something even greater; the only place on earth that is still as it should be. May we never tame it.

Andrew Denton

Once you learn to look at architecture not merely as an art more or less well or more or less badly done, but as a social manifestation, the critical eye becomes clairvoyant.

Louis Sullivan

I used to go and flatten my nose against that window and absorb all I could of his art. It changed my life. I saw art then as I wanted to see it.

Mary Cassatt

Food can be expressive and therefore food can be art.

Grant Achatz

Art should be created for life, not for the museum.

Jean Nouvel

A picture book is a small door to the enormous world of the visual arts, and they're often the first art a young person sees.

Tomie dePaola

There's no art to find the mind's construction in the face.

William Shakespeare

The capacity to be puzzled is the premise of all creation, be it in art or in science.

Erich Fromm

Love isn't an emotion or an instinct - it's an art.

Mae West

The art of life is to know how to enjoy a little and to endure very much.

William Hazlitt

We want to answer this classical question, who am I? So I think that most of our works are for art, or whatever we do, including science or religion, tried to answer that question.

Paulo Coelho

Great art is as irrational as great music. It is mad with its own loveliness.

George Jean Nathan

A race is a work of art that people can look at and be affected in as many ways they're capable of understanding.

Steve Prefontaine

Nature is the art of God.

Dante Alighieri

Like most sensible people, you probably lost interest in modern art about the time that Julian Schnabel was painting broken pieces of the crockery that his wife had thrown at him for painting broken pieces of crockery instead of painting the bathroom and hall.

P. J. O'Rourke

Poetry is the art of uniting pleasure with truth.

Samuel Johnson

The art of living is the art of knowing how to believe lies.

Cesare Pavese

Art, as far as it is able, follows nature, as a pupil imitates his master; thus your art must be, as it were, God's grandchild.

Dante Alighieri

Criticism is the windows and chandeliers of art: it illuminates the enveloping darkness in which art might otherwise rest only vaguely discernible, and perhaps altogether unseen.

George Jean Nathan

In art and dream may you proceed with abandon. In life may you proceed with balance and stealth.

Patti Smith

A beautiful lady is an accident of nature. A beautiful old lady is a work of art.

Louis Nizer

Poetry is emotion put into measure. The emotion must come by nature, but the measure can be acquired by art.

Thomas Hardy

I love having my hands in the dirt. It is never a science and always an art. There are no rules. And if it comes down to me versus that weed I'm trying to pull out of the ground that doesn't want to come out? I know I'll win.

Matthew McConaughey

Politeness is the art of choosing among your thoughts.

Madame de Stael

I have never denied my background or my culture. I have taught my child to embrace her Mexican heritage, to love my first language, Spanish, to learn about Mexican history, music, folk art, food, and even the Mexican candy I grew up with.

Salma Hayek

Smiles come naturally to me, but I started thinking of them as an art form at my command. I studied all the time. I looked at magazines, I'd practice in front of the mirror and I'd ask photographers about the best angles. I can now pull out a smile at will.

Tyra Banks

Art should be life. It's an imitation of life. It should have some humanity in it.

John Lydon

I just like art. I get pure pleasure from it. I have a lot of wonderful paintings, and every time I look at them I see something different.

Jack Nicholson

Art is contemplation. It is the pleasure of the mind which searches into nature and which there divines the spirit of which nature herself is animated.

Auguste Rodin

Art resides in the quality of doing, process is not magic.

Charles Eames

Nothing retains less of desire in art, in science, than this will to industry, booty, possession.

Andre Breton

Your talent is your art. It is not to be taken for granted.

Paula Abdul

Art has a double visage: it looks before and after. Romance is its forward-looking face. The germ of growth is in romanticism. Formalism, on the other hand, consolidates tradition; gleans what has been gained and makes it facile to the hand or the mind; economizes the energy of genius.

George Edward Woodberry

It's high time for the art world to admit that the avant-garde is dead. It was killed by my hero, Andy Warhol, who incorporated into his art all the gaudy commercial imagery of capitalism (like Campbell's soup cans) that most artists had stubbornly scorned.

Camille Paglia

The style of ancient Egyptian art is transcendently clear, something 8-year-olds can recognize in an instant. Its consistency and codification is one of the most epic visual journeys in all art, one that lasts 30 dynasties spread over 3,000 years.

Jerry Saltz

The worst state of affairs is when science begins to concern itself with art.

Paul Klee

Magic's an art where you use slight of hand or illusion to create wonder. And I was just intrigued with that idea.

David Blaine

The Dancer believes that his art has something to say which cannot be expressed in words or in any other way than by dancing.

Doris Humphrey

I'm not making art, I'm making sushi.

Masaharu Morimoto

Use the creative process - singing, writing, art, dance, whatever - to get to know yourself better.

Catie Curtis

I have trouble with modern art. But in general, all art forms fascinate me - art is the way human beings express what we can't say in words.

Andrea Bocelli

The whole aspect of cinema and film festivals should be a moment to come together and celebrate art and humanity. It would be a shame if there was such a divide.

Keanu Reeves

I quickly realized that this medium had a lot to offer someone like me. To do Disney-quality hand-drawn cartoons, you have to be a master of two art forms. Seriously, you have to be able to draw like a Leonardo da Vinci or a Michelangelo. But also you have to know movement and timing and control that through 24 frames a second.

John Lasseter

It's art that pushes against psychological and social expectations, that tries to transform decay into something generative, that is replicative in a baroque way, that isn't about progress, and wants to - as Walt Whitman put it - 'contain multitudes.'

Jerry Saltz

Acting is an art form and you want to take roles that are challenged and it's more of a challenge I think to play dark characters. Not that I want to always play those, but it is a challenge and challenges are rewarding and fun.

James Franco

Art can only be truly art by presenting an adequate outward symbol of some fact in the interior life.

Margaret Fuller

What is modern art but the attempt to pinpoint vague, incorporeal, inexpressible sensations? What is modern art, I would add, but the most solemn pile of nonsense that ever appeared on Earth?

Italo Calvino

There have to be moments when you glimpse something decent, something life-affirming even in the most twisted character. That's where the real art lies. See, I always suspect characters who are painted as lovely, decent human beings. I would always question where the darkness lies.

Martin McDonagh

When you look at art made by other people, you see what you need to see in it.

Alberto Giacometti

As a person, I was born to give out my opinions. By giving out my opinions, I realize who I am. As long as I can communicate, I'm not so lonely. If I cannot travel, or do art, or have company, if they take away all my belongings, it doesn't matter at all.

Ai Weiwei

Copy, art, and typography should be seen as a living entity; each element integrally related, in harmony with the whole, and essential to the execution of an idea.

Paul Rand

The art of coalition command - whether it is here in Afghanistan, whether it was in Iraq or in Bosnia or in Haiti - is to take the resources you are provided with, understand what the strengths and weaknesses are and to employ them to the best overall effect.

David Petraeus

I really don't like art where you need to know so much theory to understand. If the theory is removed, it doesn't do anything. That means that this work is an illustration of theory, and I don't believe in the power of the work itself.

Marina Abramovic

I just love entertaining. I will do anything - stand-up comedy, video games, fencing, internet shorts - I just want to keep being lucky enough to entertain people anyway I can. I try never to limit my art to a medium.

Matthew Gray Gubler

Art school had taught me it was far better to be a flamboyant failure than any kind of benign success.

Malcolm Mclaren

If you have good songs and a real desire to make music, the next thing to do, instead of approach record companies, is to get yourself a really good manager because then it allows you to focus on your profession of being a musician. Then they can focus on the darker art of the record label and the music industry.

James Blunt

The cinema occupies an important place in the overall development of art and literature.

Kim Jong Il

Widespread state control over art and culture has left no room for freedom of expression in the country. For more than 60 years, anyone with a dissenting opinion has been suppressed. Chinese art is merely a product: it avoids any meaningful engagement. There is no larger context. Its only purpose is to charm viewers with its ambiguity.

Ai Weiwei

As a child I was very into gadgets and machines and robots. The idea of experimenting with machines to create art was always something I tinkered with.

Reggie Watts

I felt obligated to change music to art, the same way that Galileo proved the Earth was round to the world and that the Sun did not stand still.

Phil Spector

Our best teachers do more than impart facts and figures - they inspire and encourage students and instill a true desire to learn. That's a fine art in itself.

Sonny Perdue

Art is the proper task of life.

Friedrich Nietzsche

She had lost the art of conversation but not, unfortunately, the power of speech.

George Bernard Shaw

Take care to sell your horse before he dies. The art of life is passing losses on.

Robert Frost

He who possesses art and science has religion; he who does not possess them, needs religion.

Johann Wolfgang von Goethe

My goal is to be one with the music. I just dedicate my whole life to this art.

Jimi Hendrix

Freedom in art, freedom in society, this is the double goal towards which all consistent and logical minds must strive.

Victor Hugo

Parents are usually more careful to bestow knowledge on their children rather than virtue, the art of speaking well rather than doing well; but their manners should be of the greatest concern.

R. Buckminster Fuller

Real art is basic emotion. If a scene is handled with simplicity - and I don't mean simple - it'll be good, and the public will know it.

John Wayne

Great art is the contempt of a great man for small art.

F. Scott Fitzgerald

The sadness of the incomplete, the sadness that is often Life, but should never be Art.

E. M. Forster

It is not hard to understand modern art. If it hangs on a wall it's a painting, and if you can walk around it it's a sculpture.

Tom Stoppard

I'm for mechanical art. When I took up silk screening, it was to more fully exploit the preconceived image through the commercial techniques of multiple reproduction.

Andy Warhol

People who don't like me talk about it as though I'm trash because I have tattoos. I find that insane because it's 2008, not the 1950s. Tattoos aren't limited to sailors. It's a form of art I find beautiful. I love it.

Megan Fox

For thousands of years, human beings have been obsessed with beauty, truth, love, honor, altruism, courage, social relationships, art, and God. They all go together as subjective experiences, and it's a straw man to set God up as the delusion. If he is, then so is truth itself or beauty itself.

Deepak Chopra

It's an art to live with pain... mix the light into gray.

Eddie Vedder

Love and business and family and religion and art and patriotism are nothing but shadows of words when a man's starving!

O. Henry

I am a walking piece of art every day, with my dreams and my ambitions forward at all times in an effort to inspire my fans to lead their life in that way.

Lady Gaga

I wasn't exposed to art as I was growing up, and can't recall the first time I saw a work of art. However, I remember very clearly a vision I had of a little green reindeer when I was a child, and visions emanate from the same mythical area where painting resides. Whatever the reason, I immediately felt comfortable working with visual materials.

William S. Burroughs

Art is permitted to survive only if it renounces the right to be different, and integrates itself into the omnipotent realm of the profane.

Theodor Adorno

You say a new era in art is preparing; you sensed it coming; continue your studies without weakening. God will do the rest.

Paul Cezanne

Another unsettling element in modern art is that common symptom of immaturity, the dread of doing what has been done before.

Edith Wharton

Art is like baby shoes. When you coat them with gold, they can no longer be worn.

John Updike

Piano playing is a dying art. I love the fact that I can be one guy with one instrument evoking an emotional and musical experience.

Jon Bon Jovi

A work of art is a world in itself reflecting senses and emotions of the artist's world.

Hans Hofmann

For as long as I can remember I have suffered from a deep feeling of anxiety which I have tried to express in my art.

Edvard Munch

What an artist is trying to do for people is bring them closer to something, because of course art is about sharing. You wouldn't be an artist unless you wanted to share an experience, a thought.

David Hockney

Tell me thy company, and I'll tell thee what thou art.

Miguel de Cervantes

I think art is inherently nonviolent and it actually occupies your mind with creation rather than destruction.

Anthony Kiedis

A compromise is the art of dividing a cake in such a way that everyone believes he has the biggest piece.

Ludwig Erhard

Trauma happens in relationships, so it can only be healed in relationships. Art can't provide healing. It can be cathartic and therapeutic but a relationship is a three-part journey.

Alanis Morissette

Modern bodybuilding is ritual, religion, sport, art, and science, awash in Western chemistry and mathematics. Defying nature, it surpasses it.

Camille Paglia

What was any art but a mould in which to imprison for a moment the shining elusive element which is life itself - life hurrying past us and running away, too strong to stop, too sweet to lose.

Willa Cather

Thirty-three-years-old, still creating art. It's rage, it's creativity, it's pain, it's hurt, but it's the opportunity to still have my voice get out there through music.

Kanye West

I began doing writing projects and art and design projects to explore a new way of seeing Canada. Roots is one more way of continuing this exploration. I want to present a wide-open Canadian sense of color, adventure, communication and openness that defines our country.

Douglas Coupland

Reason clears and plants the wilderness of the imagination to harvest the wheat of art.

Austin O'Malley

As I grew older, I realized that it was much better to insist on the genuine forms of nature, for simplicity is the greatest adornment of art.

Albrecht Durer

Man is unique not because he does science, and his is unique not because he does art, but because science and art equally are expressions of his marvelous plasticity of mind.

Jacob Bronowski

Writing is truly a creative art - putting word to a blank piece of paper and ending up with a full-fledged story rife with character and plot.

William Shatner

Works of art make rules; rules do not make works of art.

Claude Debussy

Salesmanship, too, is an art; the perfection of its technique requires study and practice.

James Cash Penney

But theater, because of its nature, both text, images, multimedia effects, has a wider base of communication with an audience. That's why I call it the most social of the various art forms.

Wole Soyinka

I've been lucky enough to live through all the things that are supposed to give meaning to our lives, like parenting, grandparenting, art, celebrity. All these things you expect meaning to come from, and sometimes it comes when you're not expecting it.

Alan Alda

It has taken me years of struggle, hard work and research to learn to make one simple gesture, and I know enough about the art of writing to realize that it would take as many years of concentrated effort to write one simple, beautiful sentence.

Isadora Duncan

I love rock-n-roll. I think it's an exciting art form. It's revolutionary. Still revolutionary and it changed people. It changed their hearts. But yeah, even rock-n-roll has a lot of rubbish, really bad music.

Nick Cave

The details are the very source of expression in architecture. But we are caught in a vice between art and the bottom line.

Arthur Erickson

Cats are anthropomorphised in art because they are so laid back that you automatically attribute human thoughts and feelings to them.

Jim Davis

Whether it be personal or musical, I just think I'm a walking art piece, just a ball of creativity.

Chris Brown

All art is dependent on technology because it's a human endeavour, so even when you're using charcoal on a wall or designed the proscenium arch, that's technology.

George Lucas

The essence of all art is to have pleasure in giving pleasure.

Mikhail Baryshnikov

I was going to go to a four-year college and be an anthropologist or to an art school and be an illustrator when a friend convinced me to learn photography at the University of Southern California. Little did I know it was a school that taught you how to make movies! It had never occurred to me that I'd ever have any interest in filmmaking.

George Lucas

You must thank the gods for art, those of us who have been fortunate enough to stumble onto this means of venting our craziness, our meanness, our towering disgust.

Robert Crumb

The final purpose of art is to intensify, even, if necessary, to exacerbate, the moral consciousness of people.

Norman Mailer

All art is erotic.

Gustav Klimt

Rumors sound of galleries asking artists for upsized art and more of it. I've heard of photographers asked to print larger to increase the wall power and salability of their work. Everything winds up set to maximum in order to feed the beast.

Jerry Saltz

Only in art will the lion lie down with the lamb, and the rose grow without thorn.

Martin Amis

Art has a way of confronting us, of reminding us, of engaging us, in what it means to be human, and what it means to be human is to be flawed, is to be contradictory, is to be often weak, and yet despite all of these what we would consider drawbacks, that we're also quite beautiful. Spin is the opposite.

Junot Diaz

Science is what we understand well enough to explain to a computer. Art is everything else we do.

Donald Knuth

Jazz comes from our way of life, and because it's our national art form, it helps us to understand who we are.

Wynton Marsalis

There is no philosophy without the art of ignoring objections.

Joseph de Maistre

Nature is the most beautiful thing we have. It's better than art because it's from the creator.

Olivia Newton-John

To become truly immortal, a work of art must escape all human limits: logic and common sense will only interfere. But once these barriers are broken, it will enter the realms of childhood visions and dreams.

Giorgio de Chirico

Politicians are masters of the art of deception.

Martin L. Gross

The surrealists, and the modern movement in painting as a whole, seemed to offer a key to the strange postwar world with its threat of nuclear war. The dislocations and ambiguities, in cubism and abstract art as well as the surrealists, reminded me of my childhood in Shanghai.

J. G. Ballard

Painting, sculpture and architecture are finished, but the art habit continues.

Robert Smithson

For me, acting is about the art of it and it's about being on a film set and doing your thing, painting a blank canvas.

Shailene Woodley

It is not so for art in appreciation because art is concerned with human behavior. And science is concerned with the behavior of metal or energy. It depends on what the fashion is. Now today it's energy. It's the same soul behind it. The same soul, you see.

Josef Albers

I see things like they've never been seen before. Art is an accurate statement of the time in which it is made.

Robert Mapplethorpe

Surprise is key in all art.

Oscar Niemeyer

Music embodies feeling without forcing it to contend and combine with thought, as it is forced in most arts and especially in the art of words.

Franz Liszt

With few exceptions, music has been for some centuries the art which has devoted itself not to the reproduction of natural phenomena, but rather to the expression of the artist's soul, in musical sound.

Wassily Kandinsky

Surrealism: An archaic term. Formerly an art movement. No longer distinguishable from everyday life.

Brad Holland

Art and nature shall always be wrestling until they eventually conquer one another so that the victory is the same stroke and line: that which is conquered, conquers at the same time.

Maria Sibylla Merian

Because most people are not sufficiently employed in themselves, they run about loose, hungering for employment, and satisfy themselves in various supererogatory occupations. The easiest of these occupations, which have all to do with making things already made, is the making of people: it is called the art of friendship.

Laura Riding

Our humor turns our anger into a fine art.

Mary Kay Blakely

Violin playing is a physical art with great traditions behind it.

Vanessa Mae

The work of art shows people new directions and thinks of the future. The house thinks of the present.

Adolf Loos

I wish I was better at art. I love some of the great artists of the 19th century and, compared to them, I just feel I lack this technique that they had. They have so much skill.

Hayao Miyazaki

I believe that a work of art, like metaphors in language, can ask the most serious, difficult questions in a way which really makes the readers answer for themselves; that the work of art far more than an essay or a tract involves the reader, challenges him directly and brings him into the argument.

George Steiner

We all know that the great memories of our childhood are the little triumphs - it doesn't really matter whether that was in writing, art, on the hockey field or on the football field. It's something that makes you feel - 'I can do this stuff.'

Michael Morpurgo

I'm interested in what would normally be considered the worst aspects of commercial art. I think it's the tension between what seems to be so rigid and cliched and the fact that art really can't be this way.

Roy Lichtenstein

Photographing a cake can be art.

Irving Penn

I feed on art more than I ever do on photographs. I can admire photography, but I wouldn't go to it out of hunger.

Irving Penn

When you make art, you get really invested in it. When art happens by accident and you were just along for the ride? It's way more fun.

Patrick Stump

Art shows and the institutions end up being the couriers for culture for the next generation and are an important component as well. It may seem ironic from one perspective, but I think if you look at my overall strategy, it's actually not out of step.

Shepard Fairey

Serious art has been the work of individual artists whose art has had nothing to do with style because they were not in the least connected with the style or the needs of the masses. Their work arose rather in defiance of their times.

Franz Marc

I would love to spend all my time writing to you; I'd love to share with you all that goes through my mind, all that weighs on my heart, all that gives air to my soul; phantoms of art, dreams that would be so beautiful if they could come true.

Luigi Pirandello

Art is exalted above religion and race. Not a single solitary soul these days believes in the religions of the Assyrians, the Egyptians and the Greeks... Only their art, whenever it was beautiful, stands proud and exalted, rising above all time.

Emil Nolde

If you look at the requirements for just one piece, like art, from one generation of games to the next, it will change radically. You need people who are adaptable because the thing that makes you the best in the world in one generation of games is going to be totally useless in the next.

Gabe Newell

All art is quite useless.

Oscar Wilde

The art of acting consists in keeping people from coughing.

Benjamin Franklin

I think in art, but especially in films, people are trying to confirm their own existences.

Jim Morrison

Art is not merely an imitation of the reality of nature, but in truth a metaphysical supplement to the reality of nature, placed alongside thereof for its conquest.

Friedrich Nietzsche

When thou art above measure angry, bethink thee how momentary is man's life.

Marcus Aurelius

To be able to endure odium is the first art to be learned by those who aspire to power.

Lucius Annaeus Seneca

Poetry is the art of substantiating shadows, and of lending existence to nothing.

Edmund Burke

Art is not a treasure in the past or an importation from another land, but part of the present life of all living and creating peoples.

Franklin D. Roosevelt

Art is the lie that enables us to realize the truth.

Pablo Picasso

What is Art? It is the response of man's creative soul to the call of the Real.

Rabindranath Tagore

In Art, man reveals himself and not his objects.

Rabindranath Tagore

Thou must be emptied of that wherewith thou art full, that thou mayest be filled with that whereof thou art empty.

Saint Augustine

Art is not the application of a canon of beauty but what the instinct and the brain can conceive beyond any canon. When we love a woman we don't start measuring her limbs.

Pablo Picasso

The finest works of art are precious, among other reasons, because they make it possible for us to know, if only imperfectly and for a little while, what it actually feels like to think subtly and feel nobly.

Aldous Huxley

I think having land and not ruining it is the most beautiful art that anybody could ever want to own.

Andy Warhol

I think art is the only thing that's spiritual in the world. And I refuse to forced to believe in other people's interpretations of God. I don't think anybody should be. No one person can own the copyright to what God means.

Marilyn Manson

Only through art can we emerge from ourselves and know what another person sees.

Marcel Proust

Surely all art is the result of one's having been in danger, of having gone through an experience all the way to the end, where no one can go any further.

Rainer Maria Rilke

Land really is the best art.

Andy Warhol

Life is not an exact science, it is an art.

Samuel Butler

I think most of the people involved in any art always secretly wonder whether they are really there because they're good or there because they're lucky.

Katharine Hepburn

I think most art comes out of poverty and hard times.

Willie Nelson

Art is an attempt to integrate evil.

Simone de Beauvoir

Space is the breath of art.

Frank Lloyd Wright

Emotion resulting from a work of art is only of value when it is not obtained by sentimental blackmail.

Jean Cocteau

The beginning of a friendship, the fact that two people out of the thousands around them can meet and connect and become friends, seems like a kind of magic to me. But maintaining a friendship requires work. I don't mean that as a bad thing. Good art requires work as well.

Charles de Lint

To know how to grow old is the master work of wisdom, and one of the most difficult chapters in the great art of living.

Herman Melville

The sole art that suits me is that which, rising from unrest, tends toward serenity.

Andre Gide

Art begins in imitation and ends in innovation.

Mason Cooley

I am an anarchist in politics and an impressionist in art as well as a symbolist in literature. Not that I understand what these terms mean, but I take them to be all merely synonyms of pessimist.

Henry Adams

Listen to your inner-voice: Surround yourself with loving, nurturing people. Fall in love with your art and find yourself. Music is the great communicator.

Glenn Hughes

One of the interesting things here is that the people who should be shaping the future are politicians. But the political framework itself is so dead and closed that people look to other sources, like artists, because art and music allow people a certain freedom.

Thom Yorke

Once you take yourself too seriously the art will suffer.

Maynard James Keenan

All the world old is queer save thee and me, and even thou art a little queer.

Robert Owen

The art of Peace I practice has room for each of the world's eight million gods, and I cooperate with them all. The God of Peace is very great and enjoins all that is divine and enlightened in every land.

Morihei Ueshiba

Art is much less important than life, but what a poor life without it.

Robert Motherwell

When the bright angel dominates, out comes a great work of art, a Michelangelo David or a Beethoven symphony.

Madeleine L'Engle

I like the fact that in ancient Chinese art the great painters always included a deliberate flaw in their work: human creation is never perfect.

Madeleine L'Engle

Art is dangerous. It is one of the attractions: when it ceases to be dangerous you don't want it.

Duke Ellington

Design in art, is a recognition of the relation between various things, various elements in the creative flux. You can't invent a design. You recognize it, in the fourth dimension. That is, with your blood and your bones, as well as with your eyes.

D. H. Lawrence

Let's say intelligence is your ability to compose poetry, symphonies, do art, math and science. Chimps can't do any of that, yet we share 99 percent DNA. Everything that we are, that distinguishes us from chimps, emerges from that one-percent difference.

Neil deGrasse Tyson

Politics is the art of the possible.

Otto von Bismarck

Environmental concern is now firmly embedded in public life: in education, medicine and law; in journalism, literature and art.

Barry Commoner

They teach you there's a boundary line to music. But, man, there's no boundary line to art.

Charlie Parker

Mathematics is, as it were, a sensuous logic, and relates to philosophy as do the arts, music, and plastic art to poetry.

Karl Wilhelm Friedrich Schlegel

Art is why I get up in the morning but my definition ends there. You know I don't think its fair that I'm living for something I can't even define.

Ani DiFranco

Teachers believe they have a gift for giving; it drives them with the same irrepressible drive that drives others to create a work of art or a market or a building.

A. Bartlett Giamatti

Art is magic... But how is it magic? In its metaphysical development? Or does some final transformation culminate in a magic reality? In truth, the latter is impossible without the former. If creation is not magic, the outcome cannot be magic.

Hans Hofmann

Layer by layer art strips life bare.

Robert Musil

Wit as an instrument of revenge is as infamous as art is as a means of sensual titillation.

Karl Wilhelm Friedrich Schlegel

I decided at 40 I was wasting entire chunks of my brain and didn't want to blow my one chance on Earth. I'm glad I made that decision. Writing is largely about time, while visual art is largely about space. Sometimes, as with film, you can hybridize, but I think it's basically the space part of my brain wanting equal footing with the time part.

Douglas Coupland

You can understand nothing about art, particularly modern art, if you do not understand that imagination is a value in itself.

Milan Kundera

One's art goes as far and as deep as one's love goes.

Andrew Wyeth

An art book is a museum without walls.

Andre Malraux

I view art as an inspirational tool.

Thomas Kincade

Rule of art: Cant kills creativity!

Camille Paglia

Politics is the art of the possible; creativity is the art of the impossible.

Ben Okri

Let's talk of a system that transforms all the social organisms into a work of art, in which the entire process of work is included... something in which the principle of production and consumption takes on a form of quality. It's a Gigantic project.

Joseph Beuys

The growth of art seems to be in cycles, and often its vigorous lifetime is restricted to a century or two. The periods of distinctive drama, Greek, English, Spanish, fall within such a limit; the schools of painting and sculpture likewise; and, in poetry, the Victorian age or the school of Pope will serve as examples.

George Edward Woodberry

In the 1960s when the recording studio suddenly really took off as a tool, it was the kids from art school who knew how to use it, not the kids from music school. Music students were all stuck in the notion of music as performance, ephemeral. Whereas for art students, music as painting? They knew how to do that.

Brian Eno

Art allows people a way to dream their way out of their struggle.

Russell Simmons

Gloom and solemnity are entirely out of place in even the most rigorous study of an art originally intended to make glad the heart of man.

Ezra Pound

Works of art often last forever, or nearly so. But exhibitions themselves, especially gallery exhibitions, are like flowers; they bloom and then they die, then exist only as memories, or pressed in magazines and books.

Jerry Saltz

This is part of the involuntary bargain we make with the world just by being alive. We get to experiences the splendor of nature, the beauty of art, the balm of love and the sheer joy of existence, always with the knowledge that illness, injury, natural disaster, or pure evil can end it in an instant for ourselves or someone we love.

Jeff Greenfield

'Summer of Love: Art of the Psychedelic Era,' the Whitney Museum's 40th-anniversary trip down counterculture memory lane, provides moments of buzzy fun, but it'll leave you only comfortably numb. For starters, it may be the whitest, straightest, most conservative show seen in a New York museum since psychedelia was new.

Jerry Saltz

Fine art is knowledge made visible.

Gustave Courbet

Art is always criticized and always an outsider gets the blame.

Ville Valo

The public needs art - and it is the responsibility of a 'self-proclaimed artist' to realize that the public needs art, and not to make bourgeois art for a few and ignore the masses.

Keith Haring

One can re-create what was in the mind of a mathematician a thousand years ago, recapture the truth of the intellect wherever it may have once come to light; but the image of art, that infinite variable of perception and expression in the individual, - that is not easily re-created, at least, not with certainty and in its original fulness.

George Edward Woodberry

I like it when somebody tells me a story, and I actually really feel that that's becoming like a lost art in American cinema.

Quentin Tarantino

Science, like art, religion, commerce, warfare, and even sleep, is based on presuppositions.

Gregory Bateson

The art of economics consists in looking not merely at the immediate but at the longer effects of any act or policy; it consists in tracing the consequences of that policy not merely for one group but for all groups.

Henry Hazlitt

In art, all who have done something other than their predecessors have merited the epithet of revolutionary; and it is they alone who are masters.

Paul Gauguin

Broad paths are open to every endeavour, and a sympathetic recognition is assured to every one who consecrates his art to the divine services of a conviction of a consciousness.

Franz Liszt

You are welcome to your intellectual pastimes and books and art and newspapers; welcome, too, to your bars and your whisky that only makes me ill. Here am I in the forest, quite content.

Knut Hamsun

Film as dream, film as music. No art passes our conscience in the way film does, and goes directly to our feelings, deep down into the dark rooms of our souls.

Ingmar Bergman

I make pictures and someone comes in and calls it art.

Willem de Kooning

In the end, nature is inexorable: it has no reason to hurry and, sooner or later, it takes what belongs to it. Unconsciously and inflexibly obedient to its own laws, it doesn't know art, just as it doesn't know freedom, just as it doesn't know goodness.

Ivan Turgenev

Art flourishes where there is a sense of adventure.

Alfred North Whitehead

Of course the illusion of art is to make one believe that great literature is very close to life, but exactly the opposite is true. Life is amorphous, literature is formal.

Francoise Sagan

The art of politics consists in knowing precisely when it is necessary to hit an opponent slightly below the belt.

Konrad Adenauer

I believe that my art gets across the point that I'm in this morality theater trying to help the underdog, and I'm speaking socially here, showing concern and making psychological and philosophical statements for the underdog.

Jeff Koons

Damien Hirst is the Elvis of the English art world, its ayatollah, deliverer, and big-thinking entrepreneurial potty-mouthed prophet and front man. Hirst synthesizes punk, Pop Art, Jeff Koons, Marcel Duchamp, Francis Bacon, and Catholicism.

Jerry Saltz

A work of art when placed in a gallery loses its charge, and becomes a portable object or surface disengaged from the outside world.

Robert Smithson

I don't know if One Direction will stand the test of time. I have a niece who goes crazy for them. But the only way to judge art is to wait and see if it becomes evergreen. This takes a bit of time. Adele is a very good musician and I'd like to sing with her. But, again, time will tell if her music will become evergreen.

Andrea Bocelli

The chief function of the city is to convert power into form, energy into culture, dead matter into the living symbols of art, biological reproduction into social creativity.

Lewis Mumford

I think that the first part of the art is making the art, but when art really becomes art is when it belongs to somebody else.

Pete Wentz

I never, ever had it in my mind that I wanted to be in the record industry, because I still contend that the record industry is an insidious affair. It's this terrible collision between art and commerce, and it will always be that way.

Ian MacKaye

Any fool can have bad luck; the art consists in knowing how to exploit it.

Frank Wedekind

I am one of those unhappy persons who inspire bores to the greatest flights of art.

Edith Sitwell

Anyone who relishes art should love the extraordinary diversity and psychic magic of our art galleries. There's likely more combined square footage for the showing of art on one New York block - West 24th Street between Tenth and Eleventh Avenues - than in all of Amsterdam's or Hamburg's galleries.

Jerry Saltz

When museums are built these days, architects, directors, and trustees seem most concerned about social space: places to have parties, eat dinner, wine-and-dine donors. Sure, these are important these days - museums have to bring in money - but they gobble up space and push the art itself far away from the entrance.

Jerry Saltz

To curb the machine and limit art to handicraft is a denial of opportunity.

Lewis Mumford

A rose is the visible result of an infinitude of complicated goings on in the bosom of the earth and in the air above, and similarly a work of art is the product of strange activities in the human mind.

Clive Bell

The best history is but like the art of Rembrandt; it casts a vivid light on certain selected causes, on those which were best and greatest; it leaves all the rest in shadow and unseen.

Walter Bagehot

Art is accusation, expression, passion. Art is a fight to the finish between black charcoal and white paper.

Gunter Grass

All I tell artists is, 'Do what you love. Never let anybody talk you into changing what your musical idea is just to try to get a hit, because you're chasing your tail that way. It's not going to happen, and if you're successful, you have to do it the rest of your life. Stay true to it and do it for the sake of the art.'

Gloria Estefan

When the impulses which stir us to profound emotion are integrated with the medium of expression, every interview of the soul may become art. This is contingent upon mastery of the medium.

Hans Hofmann

One of the most striking signs of the decay of art is when we see its separate forms jumbled together.

Jean-Luc Godard

There is a small world of people who are very interested in contemporary art and a slightly bigger world of people who look at contemporary art. But then there is a much larger world that doesn't realise how influential art is on things that they actually look at.

Marc Jacobs

I would say being deeply involved in the art world would help keep a young artist on track. Doing what you love, so that your focus is your artistry.

Jada Pinkett Smith

Every work of art belongs to his time. I would not paint again the Mona Lisa in the third dimension.

Alejandro Jodorowsky

There is an art of reading, as well as an art of thinking, and an art of writing.

Clarence Day

I hate studio. For me, studio is a trap to overproduce and repeat yourself. It is a habit that leads to art pollution.

Marina Abramovic

The notes I handle no better than many pianists. But the pauses between the notes ah, that is where the art resides.

Artur Schnabel

www.ingramcontent.com/pod-product-compliance
Lightning Source LLC
Chambersburg PA
CBHW071350280526

45787CB00001B/273